THE SIDLAWS

THE SIDLAWS
Tales, Traditions and Ballads

MAURICE FLEMING

Illustrated by
Alyson MacNeill

MERCAT
PRESS

First published in 2000 by Mercat Press
at James Thin, 53 South Bridge, Edinburgh EH1 1YS

ISBN: 184183 0062

BY THE SAME AUTHOR

The Ghost o' Mause and Other Tales and Traditions of East Perthshire
The Real Macbeth and Other Stories from Scottish History
Old Blairgowrie and Rattray (Stenlake Publishing)

The Mercat Press website features a complete catalogue
and details of new and recent titles, all of which can be ordered online:
www.mercatpress.com

Set in Caslon and Bembo at Mercat Press
Printed and bound in Great Britain by
Biddles Ltd, Guildford and King's Lynn

CONTENTS

Serpents, Fairies, Brownies and the Deil Himsel

On the Lighter Side

The Smugglers

On the Lighter Side

Strange Echoes

On the Lighter Side

Tales from History

On the Lighter Side

Old Customs

Old Rhymes and Sayings

On the Lighter Side

A Wheen o' Witches

On the Lighter Side

Tales of the Track

Two Ghosts

Legends of Glamis

Ballads, Songs and Poems

ILLUSTRATIONS

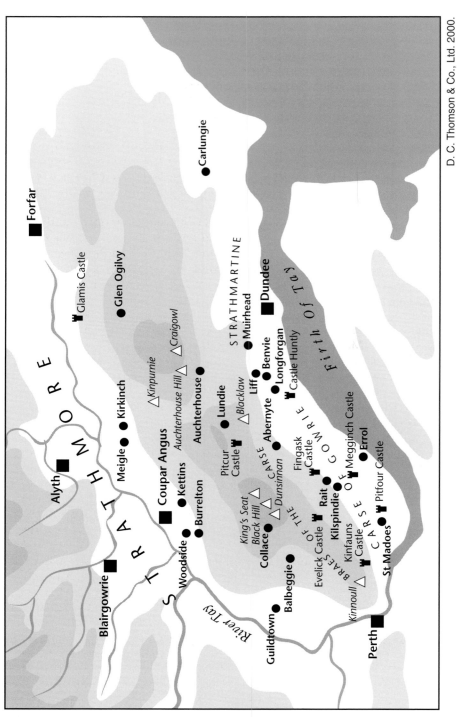

INTRODUCTION

The first time I ever set foot on the Sidlaws was when, as a small boy, I cycled out to them from Blairgowrie. My brother led the way, along first towards Alyth, then down to Meigle and on to Newtyle. At last, panting, we arrived at our destination, Kinpurnie. Throwing down our bikes we scrambled—faster than either of us could do today—to reach the top and explore the mysterious little tower which, fittingly, is the subject of the first tale in this collection.

The Sidlaws have, in a way, been a constant companion ever since—as they are to all of us who live within sight of them in Strathmore. They are our hills of home. We tend to overlook the fact that, on the other side of the range, people regard them as 'their' hills. In Rait and Kilspindie and Abernyte there is a real feeling that the Sidlaws belong to them and to all the other little communities strung along the Carse of Gowrie between Perth and Dundee.

Further north the same feeling prevails. For this is no insignificant stretch of tops. The Sidlaws start with the grand gesture of Kinnoull at Perth and continue up country towards Montrose, almost reaching the North Sea.

Considering the length of the range, and the area it occupies on the map of Scotland, the Sidlaws have been surprisingly neglected as far as the written word is concerned. You have only to look at the variety of books and other publications on such as the Cairngorms, the Pentlands and the Ochils to see that.

Perhaps their modest height has something to do with it. These are not majestic hills: there is nothing higher than Craigowl's 455 metres, yet those who know them will tell you that each of the tops has its own character and presence, marking it out from its neighbours.

The neglect on the part of writers is all the more surprising when one considers the proximity of the hills to so many towns and villages. Kinnoull and Deuchny rise from the very edge of Perth, and Craigowl, Balluderon, Balkello and Auchterhouse Hills are all within walking distance for Dundonians, as I discovered to my joy when living in the north of the city in the 1960s. Generations of Dundee youngsters and outdoor enthusiasts have made for their well-loved 'Seedlees' on fine Saturdays and Sundays. Monifieth, Forfar, Carnoustie, Brechin, Arbroath—these and many other places lie within a short travelling distance of the Sidlaws.

This book is not a guide to the hills: someone else must provide that. What I have attempted to do is track down the lore of the Sidlaws, that heady mix of history and myth which is the heritage of every corner of Scotland. When I did this in East Perthshire for *The Ghost o' Mause*, I was amazed by the number and quality of the legends and historical tales. This time I have been even more de-lighted to amass, from all sorts of sources, a kistful of old and unexpected treasures. Stories, poems, songs, ballads and rhymes—they give us, I believe, an insight into the lives of the folk of the past who lived in or close to the Sidlaws, their beliefs and fears, their hardships and fierce loyalties, and occasionally, I am glad to say, something of their humour too.

The most exciting part of the undertaking for me has been the discovery of so many splendid classic folktales all but on the verge of extinction on the ground. It would be good to think that printing them here will give a new lease of life to once popular stories such as 'The Shod Wife', 'The Green Serpent', 'The Stolen Bell' and 'The Brownie o' Errol'.

If it also reminds readers of the pioneer railway that ran through (or rather over) the hills, of the conventicles once held amongst them, and the colourful history of the castles and their families, then it will certainly have been well worth while.

I wish to express my thanks to all who have assisted me, particularly the following: Jeremy Duncan, Local Studies Librarian at the A.K. Bell Library, Perth; the staff of the Local Reference Department, Wellgate Library, Dundee; the National Library of Scotland; Simon McGowan and staff, Blairgowrie Branch Library; *The Scots Magazine* for providing the map, and John Methven and Alison Cook of that publication; *The Courier and Advertiser*; David M. Phillips, *The Blairgowrie Advertiser*; Stuart McHardy; Lady Strange, Megginch; the late Walter Courts; Miss Fothergill, the Perthshire Society of Natural Science; Archy C. Macpherson; Tom Johnstone, my editor at Mercat Press; and Pauline Isaacs and her wonderful computer.

My gratitude, too, to Alyson MacNeill for capturing the spirit of the stories with her striking illustrations. This is the third book she has illustrated for me and her touch never falters.

Maurice Fleming
Blairgowrie, 2000

Some Strange Fowk

The Hermit of Kinpurnie

From my upstairs windows I can see, away across Strathmore, Kinpurnie Hill with its little tower on the summit. In all of the Sidlaws this is one of the most distinctive landmarks. Walking or motoring, the tower is the feature people will often turn to look for to get their bearings.

The local history books will tell you that it was built as an observatory by the Hon. James McKenzie, Lord Privy Seal, a keen astronomer. There is, however, another story. The village of Newtyle lies close to the foot of the hill and there an old woman, Eppie Black, used to relate this tale.

It seems that the landowners around Dundee were up in arms about the activities of a poacher called David Gray. They knew he was stealing their game, but the trouble was their gamekeepers could not catch him at it. To be honest, they were a bit afraid of him for he was a powerful chap and none of them fancied tackling him. In any case he was a fast runner and when he was spotted he could outrun any of them.

The estates of Balunie, Camperdown and Auchterhouse were his favourite hunting grounds but he knew no boundaries and set his snares where it pleased him.

David Gray lived alone, shunning all company, and it was this side of his character that at last gave the lairds the idea of a way of getting rid of him. They were gathered one night for a dinner and the talk got round to Gray and how much they resented his stealing their game.

How could they put a stop to it and yet stay within the law themselves?

It was then one of them came up with a most ingenious plan. David Gray loved his own company, yes? Well, why not build a tower for him somewhere right away from any other habitation? Somewhere nobody would see him or bother him. Surely that would suit him admirably?

He would be required to live there alone for seven years during which time he would be provided with food and water. At the end of the seven years he would be given the sum of one hundred pounds, a lot of money in those days.

The lairds all loved the idea, but they were too clever to present it to David Gray themselves. He would instantly suspect it was just a trick to stop his poaching. Instead they would invite applications for the post as a hermit in the hope that he would be the only one daft enough to apply.

When the question arose as to where they would build the tower, there was no dissension. Everyone agreed there was one ideal spot: the top of Kinpurnie Hill. It was well away from any other houses and they could keep an eye on him there and see that he obeyed the conditions and did not leave the tower.

The lairds gladly contributed to a fund to pay for the building of the tower. There was no lack of labour on their estates and no shortage of stone. Soon the tower was up and ready for its occupant.

The Dundee bellman, or town crier, was instructed to go through the city to 'advertise' that a hermit was wanted for the brand-new building on Kinpurnie. The benefits were described at length: no rent to pay, free food, the hundred pounds when he came out. Perhaps it was also mentioned that he would have constantly before him one of the finest views in the country.

David Gray heard the bellman's announcement and fell right into the trap. He thought it would suit him down to the ground.

Poaching was hard work. Why, he asked himself, should he go on creeping about the woods at night in all weathers when he could sit and get his food for nothing? He had no friends, so being on his own up there would not be any hardship. In fact, he looked forward to the peace and quiet.

He applied and was quickly accepted. The lairds secretly rubbed their hands in glee. Some of them were there waiting on the day he climbed the hill to move in.

A bed awaited him, but that was all, there was no other furniture. There was no fireplace: to keep him warm he was given a sheepskin. The 'food' he was to live on was to be plain bread and he was not allowed to talk to the folk who brought it and passed it to him through an aperture in the wall.

Another condition was that his hair and his beard were to be allowed to grow and his finger and toe nails were also to remain uncut. Throughout the seven years he was not to be given a drop of water to wash himself.

The lairds locked the door of the tower behind him and took the key with them as they went chuckling down the hill. What with the cold and the poor diet they did not expect that Gray would live very long. He was used to a good diet of game and fish and a healthy life in the open air. Being shut up in that small cold cell would surely kill him.

They were wrong. As month followed month David Gray seemed to be thriving in his spartan conditions. The men who took him his daily bread and water reported that they often heard him pacing the floor and singing to himself at the top of his voice.

Season followed season and year followed year, and Gray was still there, always ready to take his bread and water when it was pushed through the hole in the wall.

The Hermit of Kinpurnie became quite famous and people came from far afield just to stand at the foot of the hill and stare up at his prison house.

After six years had passed the Magistrates of Dundee were so curious that they came to Newtyle and climbed up to the tower. He must have heard their footsteps for he shouted to them through the hole in the wall but they could not make out the words.

And so the final year passed and at last the great day came when his time in the tower was up. A huge crowd covered the slopes of Kinpurnie, all eager to see how David Gray looked after his seven solitary years. More than a third of the landowners

He shambled out, shielding his eyes from the bright sunlight…

who had devised the plan and paid for the tower were now dead, but all those surviving were there to see him come out.

At last the moment came. One of the lairds stepped forward and turned the key in the rusty lock. A great cheer and applause broke out as the door creaked open and then there was a breathless silence as they all waited for the hermit to appear.

He shambled out, shielding his eyes from the bright sunlight, and the crowd gasped. Seven years before, his hair and beard had been jet black. Now they were long, white and shaggy. The nails on his fingers and toes were like seagulls' claws.

He gaped at the crowd in a bewildered, fuddled way as if he did not know why they were there or what was happening, and then he could be seen struggling to speak. The crowd strained to hear what he had to say but instead of words there came out other sounds, noises like the moaning of the wind, the croak of a raven, the twittering of small birds, the bellow of a cow, the bark of a fox. All the sounds that had been his only company throughout his long seven years.

From the vacant stare in his eyes it was obvious to all that his mind had broken down.

The crowd fell back as the bent and pathetic figure was led hobbling down the hill and helped into a coach. He was driven to Dundee where doctors were engaged to care for him and nurse him back to health. The first thing that had to be done, of course, was to clean him up, cut his hair and beard and trim his painfully long nails. Then they began to reintroduce him to cooked food.

Two weeks after his release he fell into a fever and lay very ill for several months. He was nursed back to reasonable health but never recovered anything like his old physical strength. His mind failed to recover and he shrank away from anyone who came near him.

A year and a half after the door of the tower had been opened, David Gray died peacefully.

Local people used to call Kinpurnie's ruined tower 'David Gray's Castle', but no one now is left alive who remembers the hermit, one of the Sidlaws' strangest and saddest characters.

The Cannibal Girl

On the road from Muirhead to Newtyle (B954) you pass the Glack of Newtyle. A glack is a hollow or ravine—hollow is the better description here for it is a low-lying, marshy place with reedbeds, scattered trees and scrub.

This is a piece of land man has never been able to tame, somehow wilder than the hills through which you pass as you descend the road curving down to Newtyle. It is an area in striking contrast to the neat fences and trim fields behind you.

The Glack has always been a wild place, and if tradition is to be believed it was at one time the haunt of the most savage family in the history of the Sidlaws.

It was the historian Pitscottie who first told the story. Writing in the latter part of the sixteenth century, Robert Lindesay of Pitscottie recorded that 'ane brigant' attacked travellers here, not to rob them—though he no doubt did that as well—but for meat for his wife and family. He killed 'young men and children' and claimed that the younger they were the better they tasted.

In time he was hunted down by the authorities and the whole family was burned at the stake, all except a year-old baby girl.

The child was taken to Dundee where foster parents were found for her but as soon as she 'cam to ane woman's yieres' she, too, was condemned to death by burning. It is not clear if she was punished for the cannibalism of her family when she was still a child or if she had repeated the crime.

Large crowds gathered to watch her die, 'speciallie of women, cursing her…'. She rounded on them furiously, asserting that she had done nothing to be ashamed of: 'If ye had experience of eating men and women's flesh ye wad think it delicious,' she told them.

She went to the flames unrepentant.

Galloway's Sawney Bean is far more famous but it should not be forgotten that the Sidlaws, too, had their family of cannibals.

The Mean Wife

The parish of St Martin's lies between the River Tay and the north side of the Sidlaws, and Cairnbeddie is at the heart of it. Here once lived a Laird's wife who would do anything to save a copper or two.

Flax was grown on the estate and it fell to her to give it out to local women who spun it into yarn and then brought it back to her. The system was that she weighed the flax by the stone and paid them for the yarn, not with money, but with oatmeal which she measured out in a container called a lippie.

The poor women, however, never got a fair reward for their labours. She always gave them more than a stone of flax while the lippie was smaller than it should have been. She therefore cheated them twice with every transaction. Even if some of the women suspected what was going on, none of them dared to question it. You didn't make accusations against the Laird's wife in those days.

So she died, apparently without a stain on her character, and was buried in St Martin's Kirkyard.

Shortly afterwards the minister was out taking a moonlight stroll before turning in when he saw a figure moving amongst the trees behind the Manse. When he approached to see who it was he was horrified to come fact to face with the ghost of the Laird's wife.

Hastily crossing himself he asked why she was there. The ghost gave a deep sigh and answered:

> 'It is the little lippie,
>   An the heavy stane,
> Whilk gars me wauner
>   Here sae late my lane.'

Whether the minister was able to absolve her of her sins and put her troubled soul at rest does not seem to be recorded. One can only hope so, for at least she was regretting her misdoings, even if it was rather late in the day.

Hangie's Last Day

Hangmen were never popular figures, but the last one to serve the united baronies of Stobhall and Cargill was particularly disliked. It was the casual way he went about his duties that incensed local people. He just didn't seem to care who he strung up—it was all in the day's work to him. He even took a cruel pride in the number of victims he had consigned to the next world, and he was always delighted when Drummond, the Laird of Stobhall, provided him with another neck round which to twine his rope.

Folk were particularly disgusted when a young lad, the son of a poor widow, was sentenced to be hanged, not for any offence but for some supposed crime his deceased father had committed. Surely, they thought, 'Hangie' will have some regrets about this one.

Not a bit of it. He whistled and sang as he prepared his gallows and when the terrible moment came he performed his grisly task with his customary relish.

Afterwards, as he always did, he walked across the field to St Hunnand's Well by the chapel of the same name. He could be heard singing cheerfully as he bent to wash his hands at the spring.

Then, crash! There was a thunder clap and a flash of lightning. The skies turned dark and there was a rustling sound as if the four winds of heaven were all blowing at once. Some people said they heard a shriek, others said it was a laugh, but whatever it was, no one had heard the like of it before.

When it had all died down and the sky had cleared, a few of the bolder ones approached to see what had happened. The chapel was half ruined and the ground round the well torn up. Of Hangie there was no sign. He had disappeared.

Where had he gone? They never found out and he was never seen again. Some were of the opinion that he had been struck by a thunderbolt. Others believed the Devil himself had carried him off. That would account, they said, for the damage done to the chapel.

Whatever the truth, nobody missed him for it was a happier and a better place without him.

From Castles and Houses

An Angus Heroine

A strange baptism once took place in the old house of Auchterhouse. Those attending it were, from the looks of them, people of standing, yet they arrived secretly, under cover of darkness.

The child had been born two days earlier. There was no public celebration of his birth. As soon as the baptism was over, the guests departed as quickly as they had come. Not long afterwards the mother and child also left, slipping away to muted farewells.

What was going on? Who was the mother and why the mystery?

The year was 1751. She was Lady Margaret Ogilvy. As supporters of Bonnie Prince Charlie she and her husband David had been forced to flee Scotland after Culloden. They had sought exile in France. She had travelled back to Scotland in disguise to have her child and to see it baptised.

It was a journey made at great risk: had she been unmasked she would have been arrested and imprisoned. The guests at the baptism—Jacobites all—knew they, too, were risking everything by attending the ceremony.

There were, however, good reasons why Lady Margaret wanted her child born and baptised in Scotland. Aristocratic families required very full certification to prove their birth and identity. Without this they could run against all kinds of problems. She had been determined this was not to happen to her child.

No doubt sentiment came into her decision as well. Other Jacobite women were willing to give birth in foreign lands. Not her.

It was a courageous decision but typical of Margaret. When Charles had been declared Prince Regent and his father King at The Cross in Coupar Angus, it is said that she stood fearlessly by her husband's side, a drawn sword in her hand.

David joined the Prince's army in Edinburgh, where he was at once made a member of council. He had been close to the Prince all the way to Derby and was in charge of the cavalry on the long retreat back over the border.

On hearing he was back in Scotland, Margaret had hastened to Glasgow and joined him there. She insisted on travelling with him as they headed north. After Culloden she fell into English hands at Inverness. The Duke of Cumberland, hearing what a prize his men had netted, ordered her to be taken to Edinburgh Castle and locked up.

Margaret was not long there when she made a daring escape from her cell by changing clothes with her maid. It was then she slipped across to France, a perilous journey made partly in disguise. Her husband was already there, having sailed from Dundee to Bergen, and then making his way through Sweden.

After the baptism of her son David, this brave woman returned to France to rejoin her husband (it is thought he did not come with her to Auchterhouse).

Sadly, there is not a happy ending to her story. She died, still in France, six years later, aged only 33. David, the heir born at Auchterhouse, was mentally defective and not able to inherit the title and the lands of Airlie. Nevertheless, one feels Margaret would not have regretted a single thing she did and, at her death, would have looked back on her adventurous life with relish.

The Red Reiver

Long before the Grays were the Lairds of Kinfauns, the Charteris family owned the lands and passed them on from one generation to the next.

A colourful story is told of how the first Charteris came to be there, a story that has its beginnings in thirteenth-century France. There a man called Thomas de Longueville, a member of a proud old French family, had a violent quarrel with a nobleman and killed him in the King's presence.

He escaped and, from his place of hiding, appealed for a royal pardon. When this was refused he fled the country and went to sea.

He became a notorious pirate known, from the colour of his flag, as the Red Reiver or Rover. For years he terrorised shipping and might have gone on doing so for the rest of his life or until justice caught up with him.

However, in May 1301, with his pirate flotilla, he encountered a ship carrying Sir William Wallace to France. Thinking this single ship would be an easy quarry for his fleet, Thomas the Red Reiver leapt aboard followed by his murderous crew.

Next moment he was flat on his back. Wallace had knocked him from his feet and pinned him to the deck by the throat. The pirates fell back, astonished. This had never happened to their leader before.

Thomas, helpless, begged that his life be spared. Wallace rose and told him, 'I have never taken as a prisoner any man who was my foe. For God's sake, I grant you your life.'

He let Thomas keep his sword but first made him swear on it that he would never use it against him. As was the custom, the defeated man offered to take service with Wallace. Wallace declined, but ordered the pirate fleet to accompany him to France. They landed at La Rochelle where Wallace was feted by the local people as a hero.

On the voyage Wallace had grown to like and admire the pirate adventurer so now, instead of simply handing him over to the authorities, he took him to Paris and spoke on his behalf to the King.

He was so persuasive that Thomas was pardoned, not only for the murder he had committed years before but for his piracy as well. Now a free man, he accompanied

Wallace on his return to Scotland and from then on was a staunch friend to the Scottish leader and fought in his campaigns until Wallace was betrayed, captured and put to death in London.

Along with many Scots, Thomas then transferred his allegiance to the new freedom fighter, Robert the Bruce. He was with him when, in 1311, Bruce beseiged Perth. The town was held for Edward II by a Scottish turncoat, William Oliphant. For six weeks Bruce and his men waited and watched and there was still no sign of Oliphant surrendering.

Bruce pretended to have given up and withdrew his army. However, they went only a short distance. A week later, under cover of darkness, Bruce returned with a group of hand-picked men. The Frenchman was among them.

They carried scaling ladders, and when they reached the moat surrounding the town walls Bruce led his men into the water, now wading up to his chin and then swimming.

De Longueville was filled with admiration, and is said to have exclaimed, 'What shall we say of our French Lords who live at ease in the midst of feasting, wassail and jollity, when so brave a knight is here putting his life at risk to win a miserable hamlet!'

In fact Perth, even then, was much more than a hamlet but presumably the Frenchman did not know that.

He was the first to follow Bruce into the water and the next after him to set his ladder against the walls and climb to the top. The little band of warriors took Oliphant's men completely by surprise and in no time Perth was in Bruce's hands.

Bruce rewarded Thomas for his courage in the operation by gifting him the lands of Kinfauns. It seems to have been at this point that he changed his name to Charteris and was knighted. The Red Reiver, once the scourge of the seas, became a respected Scots laird.

Around 1850 a burial vault was opened under the aisle of Kinfauns church. In it was found a linen headpiece, shaped like a helmet, which was believed to have been placed on Thomas's head at his burial.

His sword was long preserved in Kinfauns Castle. It was a huge, heavy weapon for use with two hands and was described as being shaped like a broadsword with a great round knob at the upper end. Strange to think that this sword, as well as being swung in Scotland's cause, was also carried by the Red Reiver on his pirate raids.

The Bauld Pitcur

The hill farm of Tullybaccart has given its name to one of the best known passes through the Sidlaws, south-east of Coupar Angus on the A923 to Dundee. The road actually climbs at this point between the hills of Drumsuldry and Northballo but to regular users it is simply Tullybaccart.

Travelling north, motorists often stop in the lay-by at the top to admire the panorama across Strathmore to the distant hills, one of the finest views, some will swear, in all Scotland.

Just below, as they drive on, they may glimpse, on the left, the tall grey ruin of Pitcur Castle. Pitcur has suffered the same fate as another Sidlaw seat, for, like Evelick, it has farm buildings close up to its walls. It is also in poor repair.

This was the home of the Hallyburtons, an old Perthshire family who no doubt chose the site for their home because it guards a crucial route through the hills.

One of the Lairds was to become immortalised; he fought and fell supporting Claverhouse at the Battle of Killiecrankie and his name is sung every time someone launches into the great old song. This is the verse:

> The bauld Pitcur fell in a furr,
>   And Clavers got a clankie-o,
> Or I had fed an Athol gled,
>   On the braes o' Killiecrankie, oh.

I wonder how many of those who sing or hear the song today know that a 'furr' is a furrow made by ploughing, although in this context it may have been a trench separating one rig from another. A gled is a hawk.

There is a tradition that Claverhouse stayed at Pitcur the night before the battle and tethered his horse to a holly tree, which was afterwards pointed out for many years. There seems little evidence for this. A better story is that of the writer James Cargill Guthrie in *Scenes and Legends of the Vale of Strathmore*, who tells how he had a friend whose great-grandfather held the stirrup for Pitcur on the morning he mounted for the ride to Killiecrankie. The Laird's armour was so heavy that his horse's back broke only half a mile into the journey. This was taken as a bad omen, as indeed it proved to be.

On the other side of the road from the Castle and farm is a souterrain, one of the biggest and best preserved in the country, but seen, unfortunately, by very few people. The district must have supported a considerable Pictish community as other signs of early habitation have been found. 'Pit' in the name, of course, signifies a Pictish presence.

The name Hallyburton lives on in Hallyburton House, near Kettins, where the family moved when they abandoned the Castle of Pitcur to the jackdaws.

The Secret Room

Captain Drummond was a very worried man. He had to go away from home for a few days and he was expecting a messenger to arrive with important letters. It was the time of the '45 Uprising and his home, Megginch Castle, was likely to be raided at any time. If the papers fell into the wrong hands it could spell disaster for him and many others.

His sister was in the castle but she was ill and confined to her bed. She would not be able to do what was needed. He dared not trust any of the servants lest he be betrayed. There was, however, a guest staying, a young girl. After deep thought he called her to his study.

Quietly he explained the situation. Was she willing to help? There was, he said, a secret room in the castle. No one knew where it was, except himself. If the papers were put in there they would be completely safe. If she agreed, he would show her how to reach the room.

To his great relief the girl said she would do it.

'Then follow me,' he said. He led her by various staircases and narrow passages until they stood in a dark corner in a distant part of the castle.

There he bent down and lifted a heavy hidden trapdoor in the floor. A flight of steps led down into darkness. He lit a candle and led the way, holding up the candle so that she could see where she was putting her feet. At the bottom she found herself standing in a small chamber. In a corner stood a desk.

'You will put the papers in here,' he said, opening a drawer. 'They will be safe there till I return.'

The girl nodded and shivered. The room was cold. It had no window and without the candle it would be in total darkness. She was glad when he escorted her back up the steps to the passage above.

The following morning she watched Drummond ride away. He waved to her and was gone. 'Godspeed and hurry back,' she murmured.

It was the next day the messenger came. Her hand trembled as she took the papers. Making sure none of the servants saw her, she slipped away through the labyrinth of passages, a candle in her hand. At one point she nearly panicked. Was it down this stair or around that corner? She chose the stair and, with relief, recognised a door she had passed when Drummond showed the way.

At last she stood in the dark corner. Yes, there was the trapdoor. She slipped the fingertips of both hands into the narrow space between the trap and the floor-boards. It was heavy and it took all her strength to lift it upright. The staircase yawned below.

Gripping the candle tightly she began to descend. It was like going down into a cave. When she reached the bottom she hurried over to the desk and fumbled with the drawer.

She had no sooner slipped the papers into it and pushed it shut when there was a crash overhead. She swung round and held up the candle. The trapdoor had fallen back into place.

She half ran, half scrambled up the steps and pushed against it with all her might. It was stuck fast. Again and again she pushed. It would not budge.

She sat down on the bottom step. With sinking heart she realised there was no use shouting or banging on the floor above. There was no reason for the servants to be in this part of the castle. No one entered it for months on end...

When Captain Drummond returned to Megginch he found the place in turmoil. His servants were the first to tell him the terrible news. The young girl who had been staying was missing. She had just disappeared. He hurried to his sister's room: yes, it was true. One minute the girl had been there. The next she was nowhere to be found. She had told the servants to search the grounds and countryside, the slopes of the hills behind. They had found no trace of her.

Captain Drummond listened in silence. Then, 'I think I know where she is.'

He made his way quickly along the passages and down the flights of stairs. At last he stood over the trapdoor. He went down on his knees and slipped his fingernails into the thin cracks. It was tightly shut but he dragged it up.

What a relief when he saw a white face staring up from the darkness below! In a moment he was at the foot of the steps supporting the girl and helping her to freedom.

She had no idea how long she had been there. Her candle had long since burned out and she had been in complete darkness. Drummond's return was not an hour too soon.

In an interesting letter Lady Strange of Megginch tells me the family has searched for the secret room for as long as she can remember. Alas, it seems no longer to exist. 'We believe,' she writes, 'that my great-great-grandfather, Admiral Sir Adam Drummond, destroyed the room when he did considerable rebuilding to the house around 1820.'

The Drummonds supported the Government at the time of the '45 while their neighbours, the Threiplands of Fingask, were Jacobites. Despite their political differences the two households were great friends, and Lady Strange relates that, shortly before the Rising, the Threiplands invited the Drummonds to a dinner. After dining together the two families pledged to protect each other's property in the difficult times ahead.

Later, when Government troops removed various valuables from Fingask the Drummonds of the day pursued the looters as far as Arbroath and succeeded in retrieving all the stolen items and bringing them back to Fingask.

'Adam Drummond,' she says, 'was a captain in the Hanoverian Army. He was captured after the Battle of Prestonpans but escaped by clambering through a window. His younger brother, Francis, was an Army surgeon and died of wounds after the battle. I am descended from their brother Colin.'

The Rebels of Fingask

One newspaper headline called it 'The Sale Of The Centuries'. Over three days in April 1993 the auctioneer's hammer rose and fell as an accumulation of 400 years of family history was dispersed. An astonishing 2,000 lots were sold until nothing of any value was left.

The place was Fingask Castle, on a shelf of the Sidlaws near Rait, and all the items were from within its ancient walls. The rooms had been stripped, drawers emptied, every cupboard and attic ransacked. Even the tiniest and most obscure objects passed into the hands of new owners.

Not only was this one of the biggest house sales seen in Scotland for several decades, it was the most important sale of Jacobite relics dealers could remember.

No family in the country could boast such a rich collection of Jacobite memorabilia as the Threiplands of Fingask. Their drawing-room was dominated by portraits of James the Old Pretender, Princess Clementina Sobieska, Prince Charles Edward and his brother Henry. In the dining-room hung another portrait of James and there was one of Lord George Murray, General of Prince Charlie's army on his ill-fated campaign.

Prices for many of the items were high. Three miniatures of James and his sons Charles and Henry sold for £12,000. A small snuff box bearing a cameo of Charles concealed under the lid raised £18,700 and a silver dog collar inscribed with the arms of the House of Stuart was bought for £2,000. Another notable relic was an anamorphosis, a secret likeness of Charles only revealed when viewed through a special mirrored cylinder.

From an old wardrobe came a dress worn by a daughter of the house at a ball given by Prince Charlie in 1745 and there was a letter written by him, rings engraved with Jacobite messages and the customary lock of Charlie's hair (it has been suggested that he never needed a haircut so great was the demand for his curls!).

The names Threipland and Fingask were so closely linked for so long, it seemed as if the family had always been there. In fact the castle belonged to the Bruces long before the first Threipland arrived around 1600. They had come north from Peeblesshire where Threipland is an old place-name.

Nor, having acquired Fingask, was it continuously in Threipland hands, for they lost the property on more than one occasion, as we shall see. What is true is that they always regarded Fingask as their rightful home and they were faithful in their loyalty to the Stuart cause and suffered accordingly.

One of the first signs of their sympathies came in 1674 when Patrick Threipland, Provost of Perth, is thanked for his diligence in repressing conventicles, the outlawed services held by the Covenanters. For this he was knighted by Charles II and later made a baronet. His fortunes were to turn, however, and he died a prisoner in Stirling Castle.

The Rescue

Patrick Threipland's heirs did not learn from that lesson. When the Earl of Mar raised the Stuart standard at Braemar in the Rising of 1715, Patrick's son, Sir David, and grandson, also David, both answered the call.

Young David was captured crossing the Forth during a daring raid on Edinburgh. He was marched into the capital and flung in the Tolbooth. Later he was moved into a cell in the Castle.

His window overlooked a popular walk on the Castle-hill and he used to pass the time watching the citizens stroll past. One day, glancing down, he recognised a group of ladies he knew. Fortunately there were no guards about and he waved them over to below his window. Then, with hand signals, he showed them what he wanted them to do.

His heart was beating fast as he watched them move on out of sight. Would they do what he had asked? Or would they be too afraid of getting caught?

That night he stood by the window, a long piece of cord at his feet. All was quiet and he was nearly giving up hope when at last he saw a shadow on the moonlit ground far below. It was them! The ladies waved up to him and he quickly lowered the cord. Yes, it was long enough to reach them and a bit more besides.

With the cord wrapped firmly around his wrist he waited, feeling it spring and tug at the other end. At last he saw the wave of a white arm below. He pulled up the cord and a weight with it. When it reached his window he dragged in a pile of blankets.

The ladies hurried away. It was up to David now. He had already decided that, if he was to escape, so were some of his fellow prisoners. He called them in and they set to, tying the blankets together. At last the job was finished. They lowered them from the window, only just restraining themselves from cheering when it touched the ground.

They tied their end to a bar and then, one by one, made the perilous descent to the bottom of the Rock, all the time expecting to hear the shout of a guard, the rush of feet.

But no one came. The Castle was such a secure place, escapes were not expected. David and his friends crept away and then ran more boldly. They were free.

Their one aim was to rejoin the army of the Rising. They crossed the Forth and on their way across Fife they hid for the night in a lint mill. In the middle of the night some enemy soldiers burst in. To divert their attention one of David's party set fire to the lint. In the confusion that followed they made a dash for it and gave the soldiers the slip.

The First Rising

> When the King cam to Fingask
> To see Sir David and his Leddy,
> A cod's head weel made wi sauce
> Took a hunder pund to mak it ready.

The King of that old Carse rhyme was James VIII, the Old Pretender, and thanks to it we know what he and the others ate for dinner on his first visit to Fingask, and how much it cost, if the rhyme is accurate.

James had landed at Peterhead and was on his way from Dundee to Perth when, on Saturday, 7 January, 1716, he rode up from the Carse to Fingask Castle.

The Laird, Sir David Threipland, was with him and must have felt enormous pride in inviting James to his home where he was graciously received by his wife, Lady Catherine. It is recorded that the local people pressed forward as James approached the castle, eager to touch him, his horse or even a part of the harness. An old retainer, John Doig, was punished afterwards by his local kirk for showing his loyalty by kissing James's boot.

James spent the night and before he left next day he presented Lady Threipland with a beautiful filigree watch, a diamond cross and other pieces of jewellery.

A month later James was back, but this time the mood was very different. The

Rising had failed and he was in retreat, soon to return to France. As for Sir David, he was now a hunted man, penalised for his part in the Uprising by having his home and lands taken from him. Catherine, his wife, was pregnant, but he had to leave her at Fingask not knowing how she would be treated. At any time she might be turned out and made homeless.

For some weeks Sir David stayed on secretly in the district, keeping an eye on the situation. A faithful servant, David Ritchie, found shelter for him amongst the estate tenants and told him when it was safe to visit Lady Catherine. It is said that now and again the Laird risked spending a whole night at Fingask though he must have slept lightly, on the alert for discovery.

The greatest danger came from the minister of Kinnaird who suspected what was going on and tried to wrest the truth from Ritchie. He even threatened to withdraw the sacrament from him if he would not confess.

Ritchie steadfastly refused, saying, 'Very well, the sin be on your head, not mine.'

The minister then went to Lady Catherine and told her he had received reports of a strange man having been seen going into the castle at night and not leaving till morning. Was this not a disgraceful way to behave in the absence of her husband?

Poor Lady Catherine could only submit to the accusations of infidelity rather than betray Sir David.

Without the support of the faithful Ritchie, life would have been even more difficult for the Threiplands at this time. When it was all over he was given a croft in the Carse which became known as 'The Lady's Ward' (short for Reward).

In the end it became too dangerous for Sir David to stay on in the neighbourhood. He joined a group of other Jacobite refugees and, with a heavy heart, headed north, running the gauntlet of Government troops until he reached Burghead, then Caithness, from where they sailed to Orkney. There they met up with a party of French sympathisers who took them to France and safety.

Not long after he had gone, John Doig, the servant who had kissed James's boot, was on the hill behind Fingask when he saw a troop of dragoons passing down the Glen of Rait. He hurried to warn Lady Catherine. One can imagine the scene in the castle. Lady Threipland had only three months to go before the birth of her child and these soldiers were coming either to occupy her home or destroy it.

She watched from the window as the soldiers came to a halt outside the front door. Behind her a group of ladies and servants stood in an anxious huddle. They awaited the hammering on the door, the order to get out.

Instead, the officer introduced himself politely. He said he would give the occupants twenty minutes in which they could remove and conceal valuables most dear to them. Only then would he and his men enter the building.

That started a real flurry. 'Take this! Fetch that!' called Lady Catherine as the women rushed from room to room. One woman told later how she hurried to cupboards and presses, seizing things and piling them into her muslin apron. When she got outside she found that, in her confusion, she had saved only a few old candlesticks and other articles of little worth.

All the items taken out were hidden in the grounds, some of them under piles

*Cautiously she opened the door, lifted out the heavy Bible and then made
her way back over the bodies…*

of rocks. The family long preserved a silver kettle with dents in its side made by the stones piled on top of it.

The officer meanwhile was strolling on the lawn admiring the castle and the views across the Carse. One of the women overheard him remark that if the Devil himself had been made King he would have consented to be his subject rather than risk losing such a fine place.

When the twenty minutes were up he led his men inside. They crowded the hall and the womenfolk watched fearfully. However, there were no orders for them to pack and leave. The officer told them that, for the first night at least, his soldiers would sleep there in the hall. You can be sure, though, that when the women went to their rooms they locked and barricaded their doors.

In the middle of the night Lady Threipland woke and suddenly remembered that the treasured family Bible was in a press just off the hall. Written inside it were recorded the births of her children and those of previous generations. What if the soldiers found and destroyed it?

Unable to sleep for thinking of it she rose and crept downstairs. The floor of the hall was covered with sleeping bodies and she had to step over them to reach the press. Cautiously she opened the door, lifted out the heavy Bible and then made her way back over the bodies to the staircase and up to her room.

In the morning she began to get to know the officer and in conversation told him what she had done. He was thunderstruck and said that if one of his soldiers had wakened he would probably have shot her.

The dragoons remained in the castle but appear to have been well-behaved. As Lady Catherine drew nearer to the birth of her child she was far from well, and perhaps because of this, as little as possible was done to disturb her.

A few weeks after the arrival of the troops, Lieutenant General William Cadogan, Commander-in-Chief of H.M. Forces, issued this order:

> All officers and soldiers of His Majesty's Army in North Britain are hereby
> required not to commit any disorder, nor to take any goods, cattle, or corn,
> in the house or on the estate of My Lady Fingask.
>   Given at Perth, the 25th March 1716.

However, Fingask was not to be allowed to remain in Threipland hands. The Government sold it to the York Buildings Company. Fortunately the company was willing to lease it to Lady Catherine so that she was able to continue living in it.

As the time of the child's birth approached her health was precarious. The baby, a boy, was born prematurely on 26 May. The tiny, fragile infant had to be wrapped in cotton. Catherine was so weak that an Episcopalian clergyman was rushed from Perth to administer what was expected to be her last communion and to baptise the child ere it too should die.

Catherine lay behind closed curtains round her bed while the women of the house whispered amongst themselves. The priest asked what the boy was to be called. They did not know and they thought his mother was too ill to be consulted.

As they stood there anxiously muttering the curtain was suddenly dragged back and Catherine called in a strained voice but with all the strength she could muster, 'Stuart! Stuart!'

The baptism went ahead and the child was given the name that had caused the family so much heartbreak. In spite of all they had already suffered, young Stuart Threipland was to be a Jacobite from birth.

The Second Rising

Lady Catherine recovered and, following the collapse of the '15 Rising, Sir David was allowed to return to his home in the Sidlaws. The troops by this time had gone, and he negotiated a new lease on Fingask which enabled the family to live on there, paying an annual rent.

David, who had escaped from Edinburgh Castle, also came home. The family was still thirled to the Stuart cause, and no doubt messengers from France frequently paid secret visits to Fingask with news of the latest plans for another Jacobite attempt to win the throne.

Hopes now rested on Prince Charles Edward and it would be over this period that the Threiplands acquired many of their Jacobite relics.

At last their dreams seemed about to be realised. Charles landed in Moidart in July 1745 and the call went out to all Scottish sympathisers to rally to his standard and join the march on London.

It is difficult now to realise the near-hysteria that swept through Jacobite families such as the Threiplands. The womenfolk were bedazzled by Prince Charlie. Miss Christian Threipland was typical of them. Writing to a friend after seeing him at a ball in Edinburgh she let herself get carried away:

'O had you beheld my beloved hero, you must confess him a gift from heaven; but then, besides his outward appearance, which is absolutely the best figure I ever saw, such vivacity, such piercing wit, woven with a clear judgement and an active genius, and allowed by all to have a capacity apt to receive such impressions as are not usually stamped on every brain. In short, Madam, he is at the top of perfection and heaven's darling… O would God I had been a man, that I might have shared his fate of weal or woe, never to be removed from him!'

Those were reckless days. Christian seems to have been one of a number of young women who went to a party in Edinburgh. All were wearing specially made ribbons to show their loyalty to the Stuarts. No sooner had the dancing started when some officers rushed in, tore the ribbons off and swept the ladies up to the Castle where they kept them all night. When they were allowed out in the morning the women 'walked down the High Street in a body with their torn dresses, singing Jacobite songs all the way'.

The old Laird, now close on 80, had to be dissuaded from going to join the Prince, but young David went and so did Stuart, who was by this time a trained physician. Both took part in the rout at Prestonpans when the Hanoverian commander, Sir John Cope, was caught by surprise and saw his army scattered in a matter of minutes.

David, alas, was over-zealous. Seeing a party of dragoons in flight he rode in pursuit. He followed them doggedly for about two miles whereupon they stopped, wheeled round and shot him dead. He was buried where he fell. Years later Sir Walter Scott visited the spot as a boy.

'I remember,' he wrote, 'sitting on the grave, where the grass grew rank and green, distinguishing it from the rest of the field. A female of the family then residing at St Clement's Wells used to tell me the tragedy of which she had been an eye-witness and showed me in evidence one of the silver clasps of the unfortunate gentleman's waistcoat.'

About a year after David's death, the Fingask land steward was at a horse fair in Perth when he spotted a black charger that looked familiar. On close inspection he realised it was David Threipland's, the one he had been riding on the day he died. The horse was purchased and cared for to the end of its life.

The loss of his elder brother did not weaken Stuart's resolve to play a full part in the Rising. Perhaps it was even strengthened. He was one of the loyal supporters who stayed with Charles all the way to Derby and then turned with him on the retreat north.

It used to be said in the family that when old Sir David heard the Prince was back in Scotland he called for his boots and started to pull them on. The effort was too much and he collapsed and died.

Stuart was now the head of the family, but little good it did him when, after Culloden, he was a fugitive in the heather. His adventures then, if we knew them, would fill a book.

He told afterwards how, on one occasion he was alone and going in a certain direction when he had a presentiment of danger. He changed course and it led him to a group of friends and fellow Jacobites. Later he learned that had he stuck to his original route it would have taken him straight into the arms of Government troops.

There was a painting depicting this incident at Fingask, done by a French artist, Delacour, who was living and working in Edinburgh around 1760. It showed a winged guardian warning Stuart of the danger ahead.

His medical knowledge was much sought after by his comrades living rough, and it is said that the Prince himself had cause to be grateful for Stuart's care and advice. He was certainly responsible for treating the wounds of Donald Cameron of Lochiel who, after Charles, was the most sought-after man in the Highlands. Stuart was one of a small and trusted band who accompanied Lochiel on a long and arduous escape route. Locheil had been wounded in both legs and needed skilled medical attention.

It is clear Charles held Stuart Threipland in high regard. One of the last things he did before he sailed from Scotland was to write letters to Cluny, chief of Clan Macpherson, and to Stuart, begging them to disburse money to followers most in need of it. Earlier, Stuart is said to have been one of those entrusted with the concealment of a hoard of French coins sent over to aid the Rising.

He was with the Prince when he hid out for a time with Lochiel, Cluny Macpherson and Allan Cameron, in the secret place on Ben Alder known as Cluny's

Cave. It was while they were lying low there that an amusing incident occurred. Stuart had made a haggis for the day's meal. To give it more flavour and help it go round he had added bits of apple. They were all looking forward to the treat but at the last moment it slipped through his fingers and bounced down the hillside, scattering the precious contents amongst the rocks. There was no dinner for anyone that day.

This is one of a number of stories and scraps of reminiscence told to the Edinburgh writer Robert Chambers when he visited the family at Fingask in 1853.

One other glimpse we get of him at this time is when he was in Badenoch with Lochiel and members of Clan Macpherson. A messenger brought word that there was great suffering in Lochaber as a result of the destruction wreaked by the Duke of Cumberland's forces. Could anyone help?

Lochiel opened his purse and gave all the money he could, and one of those present recorded that Stuart Threipland handed over five guineas, almost all he had. The man who told the story, Macpherson of Breakachie, quoted Stuart as saying, 'I have not so much to myself. But then, if I be spared, I know where to get more, whereas these poor people know not where to get the smallest assistance.'

There was no future for any of the Jacobite fugitives in the Highlands. Stuart managed to make his way to Edinburgh where a friendly bookseller, William Gordon, gave him sanctuary. Gordon was going on a business trip to London. Stuart put on the clothes of an assistant in the trade and went with him. From London he escaped to France just as his father had done before him.

He joined a colony of exiled Jacobites in Rouen and lived there until an amnesty was issued from London in June 1747. He then, at last, returned to Fingask.

His mother and sisters were still there, but things had been worse for them than in the first Rising. In February 1746 one of the sisters, Effie, sat down and wrote this anxious message to their neighbour, Colin Drummond of Megginch:

> Just now there is one from Perth informs us that he heard there was to be a party of Dragoons at this house this night or early tomorrow morning, in order to rase it to the bottom, and, for ought he knew, would carry my Mother, my sisters and me prisoners… which must inevitably kill my mother in a few hours.
>
> I would therefore entreat your father would give us his advice and at the same time if it were possible you would come at this time this length yourself. I have not let my mother know this report till we see if anything happens. Your father's and your advice at this juncture and assistance will very much oblige all that's here.
>
> Euphame Threipland.

Whether Colin Drummond acted on this desperate plea or not, I do not know. Dragoons did invade Fingask. They seem not to have harmed Lady Catherine or her daughters, but they inflicted great damage. Many of the fine furnishings were deliberately smashed, including the ornate bed in which the Old Pretender had slept and a beautiful satinwood harpsichord. Bedclothes were stabbed and tapestries pierced through as the soldiers rampaged from room to room searching for anyone in hiding. Spotting a tall French umbrella—then a rarity in Scotland—they attacked it savagely, thinking it was a rebel standard.

So it was to a poorer house that Sir Stuart returned. The family fortunes were at a low ebb but the Threiplands were a gutsy lot. Stuart made a good marriage and moved to Edinburgh where, setting up as a doctor, he built up a strong practice.

Back at Fingask the Dowager Lady and Effie showed themselves more than capable of restoring the castle and estate.

When a sale of forfeited lands was held in August 1783 Sir Stuart placed a bid for Fingask and Kinnaird. It was the only offer and it was accepted. What a day of rejoicing that must have been for the Threiplands and their friends!

For a time there was one fly in the ointment at Fingask. Effie had taken a kindly interest in a herd-boy who was brought into the household as a servant. She had helped to educate him and he rose to become estate factor.

Unfortunately McDougal grew arrogant and began to behave as if the estate was his, felling trees without permission and even, at one point, ordering alterations to be made to the castle itself.

McDougal went too far on the day he rode over to the neighbouring castle of Evelick and asked for Sir Alexander Lindsay's daughter in marriage. Sir Alexander promptly kicked him downstairs.

Eventually there was a lengthy law suit involving Sir Stuart and McDougal over property which the factor claimed was his. Sir Stuart won the suit in the end and McDougal was rendered penniless, dependant on the Laird's benevolence.

Stuart Threipland was now prospering. His castle and estate were in good heart and he had a fine home in Edinburgh where he mingled in the best of company. But he could never forget his times of privation in the Highlands. Once, when a maid was going to great pains to smooth his bed, he told her not to trouble, remarking that at one time he had slept for months on heather with stones for his pillow.

Despite becoming one of Edinburgh's most solid citizens he remained an unrepentant Stuart supporter. Jacobites down on their luck—and there were many —could depend on him for help and, according to Robert Chambers, the first glass of port was always drunk 'To the Land of Cakes—and the right "Steward" to deal them!'

Chambers also relates that 'when the news of the peace of Amiens was imported to him by a servant, he was heard to murmur, "There'll never be peace till Jamie come hame".'

He died at his beloved Fingask in February 1805 aged 89, a highly respected senior member of the Royal College of Physicians, Edinburgh.

However one thing had not been done—the Threipland baronetcy had not been restored. It was Stuart's son, Patrick, who succeeded in retrieving it. When George IV made his famous visit to Edinburgh in 1822, Patrick put in a plea that the attainder be lifted. It took four years for it to happen but at last it did. There were great celebrations at Fingask. Charles Spence, the local poet, wrote a song for the occasion and it was sung at the celebration on the night of 11 May 1826. I give the first lines:

(to the tune 'There's Nae Luck Aboot The Hoose')

O light a blaze on Fingask braes,
Set a' the whins alowe,
And wave a flag o' blue and red
Upon the Jessie Knowe.
Ca' a' the neibors to a feast,
And gar them drink their fill;
Wi' loud huzzas the echoes raise
And let us joyful be,
And let us joyful be,
Our Laird is now a Knight again,
Huzza! Wi' three times three!

But still the Threiplands were not cured of their Jacobitism. In the late nineteenth century, if strangers called at the castle, two passwords were asked of them: first, 'Are you Jacobites?' and second, 'Are you Good Tories? Not Conservatives, we must have the real thing.'

These questions having been satisfactorily answered, the various antiquities and relics from their rebel past would be produced and shown with pride.

The Threiplands stayed on at Fingask until 1917 when it was sold, with Kinnaird, to Sir John Henderson Stewart (at least he had the right surname!). After his sudden death in 1924 the estates were bought by a Dundee jute merchant called Gilroy. It was to be 1968 before the Threiplands again entered Fingask, recovering the treasures they had left there.

The 1993 sale looked like being the end of the family's association with the old house. Mr Mark Murray Threipland and his American-born wife had decided that they wanted to live in Lucca, Italy, instead.

'Fingask is a lovely place,' he was quoted as saying, 'but it's time to give someone else the pleasure of living in it. It's the practical thing to do.' To another newspaper reporter he said that he and his wife just wanted to sit in the sun, adding that his son, 'had more brains than to pour all his money into this old place'.

He said he was glad that many of the items had found new homes in Scotland and that some at least would be on view to the public in museums and galleries.

The Threiplands left for Italy £1.3 million richer. In their baggage was a set of Scottish eighteenth-century wine glasses, the only heirloom they retained from the family's once great treasure house.

But that was not, after all, the last chapter in the history of the Threiplands and Fingask. The surprise purchaser of the empty building was Andrew Threipland, brother of the previous owner. When he moved in he even brought with him a number of old family items he had bought at the sale. I can imagine the Threiplands of the past nodding and smiling their approval.

And perhaps the Fingask ghosts, too. There are said to be two: a lady in white, who searches for something lost in an upstairs room, and someone downstairs who rearranges the furniture.

The Gifts

The streets of Perth were deserted. No one was venturing out of doors. The reason? A terrible plague had hit the community and was spreading like a hill blaze. The only folk to be seen were the 'cleansers' who came round the streets with a cart, preceded by a man with a bell. A householder would hail them and they would go into the house, bring out a body and add it to the pile on the cart to be taken away for burial.

The cleansers were all folk who had had the plague and recovered. It did not strike the same person twice so they were safe from infection. When a whole family died they would return later to the empty house and take away goods and possessions nobody else would touch.

In the villages of the Sidlaws they spoke of what was happening in Perth in hushed tones. The plague had not spread into the countryside and folk were making sure they had no contact with anyone or anything from the city.

At Fingask Castle lived a beautiful young girl. One day a small box was delivered for her. Puzzled she opened it, then cried with delight.

Inside nestled exquisite silk ribbons and silver ornaments to hang around her neck. She wasted not a moment in trying them on. They matched her beauty perfectly.

Only hours later she felt the first symptoms of the plague.

Did she know who had sent the fatal gifts? I cannot tell. What she does seem to have realised was that someone, bearing her ill-will, had deliberately infected the items and sent them to her.

As the disease tightened its grip she called for her pony and, while she still had the strength, mounted and rode off swearing she would 'smeek' (infect) the folk of Perth.

The path she took was one that led along the hills to the city. She got as far as the western slope of Shandrie Hill before she fell to the ground and died.

When her body was discovered, a grave was dug on the spot and she was laid in it, just as she was, with neither shroud nor coffin. The ribbons and ornaments were buried with her.

A grassy mound used to be pointed out as the spot where she lay and, according to Melville in *The Fair Land of Gowrie,* it was opened up three times but nothing was found to verify the truth of the story. Perhaps it is just as well.

The Bonny Hay

The Hays, Lord High Constables of Scotland, were for long a powerful family in the Carse of Gowrie where they held lands below the Sidlaws for generations.

One of the oldest stories told of them concerns a beautiful daughter of the household, 'The Bonny Hay'. She had fallen in love with the Lord of Atholl, her father, John of Errol, approved the match and they were to be wed. She was living for the day when she and her sweetheart would exchange vows and she would go and live with him in his castle in the north.

However, it so happened that the King, Gregory, was at that time looking for a wife. He called his nobles together and asked their advice. Where could he find a suitable bride fit to be his Queen?

The nobles at once sang the praises of their own daughters. If these men were to be believed they all possessed daughters of superb beauty, charm and wit, any one of whom would make Gregory an ideal Queen.

Only one of the nobles did not press his family's claims, though he had more than one delightful daughter at home. Instead, Douglas of Dale told the King that John of Errol was the father of the most beautiful girl in the Kingdom. Without doubt, said Douglas, she was the queen the King was searching for.

So King Gregory sat down and wrote to John of Errol informing him that he wished to wed the Bonny Hay.

When he read the letter John of Errol was extremely flattered. To think the King wanted *his* daughter for a wife! Of course she was betrothed to the Lord of Atholl, but that match could easily be broken. She would soon forget him when she knew the King wanted her to be his Queen.

When the Bonny Hay heard the news she was horrified. She pleaded with her father and tried all she could to reason with him and make him understand that her heart belonged to Atholl.

It was to no avail. Her father was determined that she should marry the King.

Meantime, Gregory decided to send one of his courtiers to fetch his future bride and bring her to him. He looked around and spotted Atholl. He was a trusted man, so the King called him over and told him what he had to do.

Atholl, of course, was thunderstruck. But he had no choice; one did not argue with the King. With heavy heart he set off to do the King's bidding.

John of Errol was looking out of his castle window when he saw Atholl approaching. Thinking he was going to cause trouble, maybe even try to steal his sweetheart away, John ordered the gates to be slammed in his face. It took Atholl some time to convince John that he had been entrusted by the King to bring the Bonny Hay to his palace.

As for the Bonny Hay her heart was singing for she was sure that her lover would take her, not to the palace, but to his home in the north.

She could not believe it when they set off in the direction of the palace. She was struck dumb with misery and disappointment and they exchanged not a word on the journey.

When they reached the Court the poor girl was led before the King. He saw at once that Douglas had not exaggerated: here was a maiden of rare beauty and charm. She would be a fit partner for him and make a lovely and popular Queen.

He was, however, a little disappointed by the coldness of her manner. This puzzled him. He could not understand why it should be. Still, he put it out of his mind and, rising to his feet, announced that preparations for the Royal Wedding should begin at once.

The day of the wedding arrived and all the nobles gathered in the great hall to watch. The Abbot stood ready to perform the ceremony. The King entered and waited for his bride. When she was led in, her eyes were cast down. Then she raised them and looked around the sea of faces. She was searching for just one face, and at last she found it. Atholl was there and he was gazing at her with the very same look: one of pure love.

The King saw it. He glanced from one to the other and understood. At once, and before the startled Court, he beckoned Atholl over, joined the hands of the two lovers and told the Abbot to wed them.

And so the Bonny Hay and the Lord of Atholl became man and wife as they had so long dreamed of doing. That very night she went with him to the home he had promised her in his castle in the north. There they lived happily for the rest of their lives.

As for King Gregory he learned that Douglas of Dale had a beautiful daughter called Madeline. He met and wooed her and she fell in love with him and became his Queen and reigned by his side for many long years.

A Dawn Raid

At the end of the sixteenth century a feud broke out between Harry Lindsay, Laird of Kinfauns, and the Cochranes of Pitfour Castle, St Madoes.

Things came to a head when, in the early hours of a June morning, Lindsay set out from Kinfauns at the head of forty armed men. As they neared Pitfour all talking ceased and they moved as silently as possible in order to take the Cochranes by surprise.

There was a surprise awaiting the Lindsays, however: the gates were firmly closed and there was no way in.

Lindsay whispered to his men to lie low in the grounds. He then sent a boy to knock on the gates and ask for entry, saying he had a letter to deliver.

The boy did so and the gates were opened. At once the Lindsays rushed forward. They were not quick enough and the gates were slammed in their face.

Furious, the Lindsays attacked the gates and smashed them open. They poured into the castle, running from room to room, stealing and looting.

Cochrane's wife and nine children had been asleep. They were roused from their beds and driven outside. When they went to shelter in a barn they were driven out of there as well and had to go into the open fields.

Nor were they allowed to return. Lindsay sent word to other enemies of the Cochranes and invited them to come and stay at Pitfour, which some of them did.

Cochrane appealed for help to the King and Privy Council. The case for the two sides was heard and Harry Lindsay was ordered to withdraw the intruders from the castle and restore all stolen goods.

Surprisingly, there is no word of any other punishment for the wrongdoers and one can only imagine in what sort of state the Cochranes found their home when at last they were able to return to it.

It was only the beginning of the family's misfortune. The castle had to be sold in the first half of the seventeenth century and the Cochranes sank in the social scale. According to William Marshall in *Historic Scenes in Perthshire*, they were reduced 'to the class of cottars... the last of them died in this condition in the parish of Errol'.

The Tiger Earl

The ruins of Finavon Castle are still there, which is just as well, for an old rhyme says,

> 'When Finavon Castle runs to sand
> The world's end is near at hand.'

Finavon (sometimes spelled Finhaven) is at Oathlaw, between Forfar and Brechin. It was the seat of the Crawfords and the home in particular of the notorious Earl Beardie, the Tiger Earl, who sits playing an endless game of cards with the Devil in the recesses of Glamis Castle.

Always hot-headed, he took a leading role in a revolt against James II in 1452. The Earls of Douglas and Ross joined him, as did the Laird of Balnamoon, but it was chiefly Beardie's doing, and he bullied and cajoled many to support him who really had no heart for it.

They met the King's forces under their commander, Huntly, at Haer Cairn, near Brechin, and might have won the day had not Balnamoon switched sides. Since he had three hundred of the finest fighters on the field, the rebels stood no chance without them. It seems that Balnamoon had asked Beardie for promotion within the combined force and been refused, hence his defection to the other side.

Beardie's brother died in the slaughter, as did many men of Angus who had been pressed into service by the two Crawfords.

Beardie retired to his stronghold of Finavon to lick his wounds. Before the year was out he had led his men on revenge raids on Balnamoon and others who had turned against him.

These attacks reached the ears of the King, who decided it was time to cut this lawless Earl down to size. In April 1453 he set off for Finavon at the head of his army with the avowed intention of razing the castle to the ground. He vowed he would, with his own hands, 'make the highest stone of it the lowest'.

Hearing of this threat, Beardie knew he had gone too far. He sent James abject apologies for his misdeeds and promised to be his most loyal subject from that day on.

The King relented. However, when he arrived at Finavon he reminded Beardie of his vow. Being a King he must keep it.

He asked leave to climb to the top of the Castle. There he lifted one of the highest-placed stones and with both hands threw it to the ground far below, shouting, 'Behold my promise true!'

He then descended the stairs, shook hands with Beardie, and departed.

Earl Beardie's temper made him feared throughout Angus. One unfortunate who suffered at the hands of his wrath was a gillie from the neighbouring Castle of Careston, Jock Barefoot. Jock was sent to Finavon with a message from his master. When he arrived he spotted a magnificent Spanish chestnut in the courtyard. Taking his knife he cut himself a stick from it.

He did not know that the tree was Beardie's pride and joy. When Beardie was told what Jock had done he flew into a terrible rage and ordered that Jock be hung from a branch of the tree he had dared to touch.

Immediately after the hanging, the tree, which had been very healthy, began to decay. It lasted, however, until 1740 when a hard frost finally killed it. It was blown over in a storm twenty years later.

The tree is gone but the ghost of poor Jock is said still to be walking the road between Careston and Finavon and he is remembered in this prophecy:

> Earl Beardie never will dee,
> Nor puir Jock Barefoot be set free,
> As lang's there growes a chestnut tree.

Despite the Tiger Earl's violent life he died in bed after catching a fever in 1454. He was buried in Dundee. Through his daughter he was an ancestor of Henry Stuart, Lord Darnley, the doomed husband of Mary, Queen of Scots.

The Evelick Murder

On the map the hill road from Kilspindie up to Evelick looks like a very badly bent hairpin. It is narrow and steep and the huddle of buildings that is Evelick Farm come on you suddenly at the side of the road.

'At your own risk,' said the woman working in the yard when I asked if I might look at the tall ruin alongside the house and steadings.

I could see why she said it. The walls were in a precarious condition. There were fallen stones inside and out and more ready to topple. It was desperately in need of stabilising.

These bleak, grey stones once enclosed a happy home. Later they witnessed tragedy, a tragedy that to this day has never been satisfactorily explained.

Evelick was the seat of the Lindsays, and one of them, Sir Alexander, brought two wives here, a Fotheringhame who gave him two sons and two daughters, and then, after her death, Rachel Douglas, the widow of an advocate and poet. Rachel had a son and two daughters by her first marriage so there were now several young people in the castle.

The heir to Evelick was Sir Alexander's elder son, Thomas, who was approaching nineteen. James Douglas, Rachel's son was about the same age.

One lovely June evening in 1682 the two stepbrothers were at nearby Pitroddie Den, a steep ravine down which runs the Pitroddie Burn. Why they went there, what they were doing, we do not know, but James stumbled back to the castle alone and in a terrible state. His clothes were dirty and wet, his face and hands filthy and stained with blood. He was hardly able to speak but when they made out what he was saying it was horrific news: he said he had found Thomas lying dead in the burn from stab wounds.

Sir Alexander and some of the servants rushed to the Den. Sure enough there was Thomas's body lying across the burn in a mess of blood and mud. They carried him home and as the family wept and consoled one another the dead youth's father plied James Douglas with questions.

James insisted he had found Thomas lying dead and he had no idea who had done it. A search party was formed and set out to hunt down the murderer. They searched up and down Pitroddie Den and all round about but found no one.

At dawn James's mother and stepfather went back to see him. They demanded the truth. And now he broke down and confessed. He had done it himself. He'd had a knife with him and he had stabbed Thomas and fought with him, battering him until he was dead.

Evelick was now a place of anguished mourning. Relations between the young Lindsays and the young Douglases could never be the same again. The strain on Sir Alexander and his wife Rachel was terrible.

James was arrested and taken to Perth. In the Sheriff Court the charge against him was read out:

> That he did conceive ane deadly hatred and evil will against Thomas Lindsay, son to Sir Alexander Lindsay of Evelick, with a settled resolution to bereave him of life; he did upon the thirteenth day of this instant month, being Tuesday last, about seven hours in the afternoon or thereby, as he was coming along the Den of Pitroddie, in company with the said Thomas Lindsay, fall upon the said Thomas, and with his knife did give him five several stabs and wounds in his body, whereof one about the mouth of the stomach, and thereafter dragged him down the brae of the Den to the burn, and there with his feet did trample upon the said Thomas lying in the water, and as yet he not being satisfied with all that cruelty which he did to the said Thomas, he did with a stone dash him upon the head, so that immediately the said Thomas died.

It was a damning indictment, based upon James's own confession, but now came a shock: James stood up in court and denied every word of it!

He went back to his first story that he had found his stepbrother dead in the burn. He explained the state of his own clothes by saying he had slipped and fallen while trying to pull the body clear of the water.

And the confession he had made? He claimed he had been so shocked and frightened by the gruesome discovery that he had not been thinking straight.

In vain he was reminded of exactly what he had told his father and stepmother at dawn on Wednesday. It had been written down at his dictation:

'I have been over proud and rash all my life,' he had begun. 'I was never yet convinced there was a God or a devil, a heaven or a hell, till now.' And then: 'To tell the way how I did the deed my heart doth quake and my head rives.

'As I was playing and kittling at the head of the brae, I stabbed him with the only knife which I had and I tumbled down the brae with him to the burn. All the way he was struggling with me, while I fell upon him in the burn, and there he uttered one or two pitiful words.'

James had laid his knife on the table in front of him as he spoke and had concluded, 'The Lord Omnipotent and all-seeing God learn my heart to repent.'

That had been clear enough. Now he said it was all untrue. It threw the legal process into disarray. The trial, due to start almost immediately, had to be postponed. The fact was that, without his confession, there was no evidence to prove he had done it.

He was kept in custody and over the next four days various people appealed to him to renew his confession. Among them, not surprisingly, was his mother, thoroughly ashamed of what he had so obviously done.

It was she who at last persuaded him to tell the truth. He handed her his declaration of innocence and told her to burn it.

A cousin of the dead boy, when he heard the news, wrote a sympathetic letter to Lady Rachel:

> …The truth is, madam, there is none of us but are grieved to the bottom of our hearts that we should be obliged to pursue your son to death; but we keep evil consciences if we suffer the murder of so near a relative to go unpunished; and his life for the taking away of the other's is the least atonement that credit and conscience can allow… His dying by the hand of justice will be the only way to expiate so great a crime, and likewise be a means to take away all occasion of grudge, which otherwise could not but continue in the family.

The way was now clear for justice to take its course. It moved swiftly in those days. James threw aside his denials of guilt on 25 June. On 11 July he stood in the dock in Edinburgh. The public prosecutor, the King's Advocate, was Sir George Mackenzie, known to the Covenanters, because of his harshness, as 'Bluidy Mackenzie'.

No time was wasted. James pled guilty and was sentenced to be beheaded on 4 August.

The prisoner was led from Court and taken back to his cell in the Tolbooth, the infamous 'Heart of Midlothian' whose site is spat upon today by passersby in the High Street.

But there were still a couple more twists to come in this strange tale. James was no sooner in his cell than he made another confession. He said he had been in Edinburgh in January of that year and while there he had stolen books from a lawyer's rooms and then set fire to the place.

The lawyer, Henry Graham, was sent for and he confirmed that there had been a fire at his chambers which had destroyed the papers of clients and damaged an apothecary's next door.

It seems likely that James had been attached to Graham's office in order to train for the law. He had perhaps stolen the books and then set fire to the place to cover up the theft.

Here a bit of legal skulduggery came into play. Fire-raising was a treasonable offence. If James were to be convicted, his inheritance would be forfeited. It could be claimed, perfectly legally, by Mackenzie himself, and his crony, the Marquis of Douglas. They well knew that a considerable sum was at stake, at least £2,000. If Mackenzie ignored the arson charge and proceeded with the beheading, the money would be inherited by James's sisters. Mackenzie saw it would pay him to postpone the execution and convict him on the arson charge.

James was back in court on 9 August. He had another surprise up his sleeve. After talking to friends he had decided neither to admit nor deny the fire-raising charge. In effect he told his accusers, 'Prove it!'

There ensued a great deal of legal wrangling. Sir George Mackenzie was furious and he showed it in typical fashion, shouting at and threatening the jury.

His tirades were of no avail. It seems they saw what Mackenzie was up to and were not prepared to find James guilty of arson and so deprive his sisters of the £2,000. They declared him innocent of the charge. The verdict earned them another tonguing from Mackenzie who 'stormed and swore he would have them all imprisoned and fined and declared infamous'. In fact he did none of these things.

There was no reason now to delay James's execution any longer. It took place at the Cross on 16 August when the famous guillotine known as the Scottish Maiden performed the terrible deed.

Some questions remained unanswered, principally why did James kill his step-brother? Was it simply jealousy because Thomas was heir to Evelick, or was there some fierce argument between them which led to blows and then to bloodshed? Was it premeditated or the result of a flare-up of temper?

Throughout the whole sorry business James showed himself to be unstable, a liar whose account of anything was not to be trusted. He brought dishonour on his mother and sisters and heartbreak to the Lindsays.

Pitroddie Den keeps its secrets and if a sadness, an oppression, clings to the gaunt skeleton of Evelick Castle, it is not at all surprising.

On the Lighter Side

The Laird's Fall

A Carse of Gowrie laird had a very low opinion of the men who worked his land. In his eyes they were too stupid to do anything right. One day, in a fit of exasperation he was heard to say that he could make better workers with his own hands out of the clay in his fields.

Word of this outburst got around and resentment simmered. His men went about their daily tasks with darkened brows.

One night the Laird was riding home across the fields when his horse stumbled. He was thrown over its head and landed in a quagmire. As his legs sank in the mud he shouted for help at the top of his voice.

One of his ploughmen, plodding back from a day's toil, heard the shouts and went to investigate.

'Oh, it's you, Laird,' he said. 'I see you're busy makin' your men. Aweel, I'll no disturb ye.'

He plodded on, leaving the Laird still stuck fast.

The Laird was a much quieter man after his experience, while his workers, every time they saw him, could not stop from bursting into laughter.

Night Shifts

Sir William Nairn, Laird of Dunsinnan, was well known for his meanness. One of his ways of saving money was that he had only one bed so that he could not invite anyone to stay.

One of the few friends to call on him, George Dempster of Dunnichen, was in the house one evening when a thunderstorm broke. To Sir William's dismay Dempster told him he would have to stay the night.

In vain Sir William dropped hints that it would be better to brave the weather and hurry home. Dempster was adamant.

At last Sir William burst out, 'Well, George, if you *will* stay, you must go to bed at ten and rise at three, and then I shall get to bed after you!'

All Change

At one time Dunsinnan estate passed into the hands of a man called Mellis. On receiving the property he changed his name to Nairn, the Dunsinnan family name.

Two men were heard discussing the change of ownership and one remarked that the new Laird was well spoken of.

'He ought to be,' responded the other, 'since he has laid aside "malice" and is "done sinnin!"'

After Midnight

In the middle of the eighteenth century the Minister of Inchture was a Mr Randall. His parishioners called him 'Mr Randie' though I have no reason to believe that anything should be read into that!

He was a fanatic in making sure that his flock did nothing they shouldn't on the Sabbath Day, and for him this started at twelve o'clock on Saturday night.

When midnight struck on Saturday he would often set out from his manse to walk round the village on the lookout for anyone still about and listening for sounds of unseemly revelry. Music, singing and any other kind of frivolity was forbidden as was any sort of work. By twelve o'clock he expected everyone to be in bed and asleep.

It was therefore something of a shock one dark night when, well after midnight, he saw a light in the distance. Someone was still up! He approached the cottage and peered in at the window. What he saw made the eyes pop out of his head. A woman was standing at the kitchen table making bannocks.

He strode to the door and burst in.

'Oh, woman, woman, you're breaking the Lord's Day! Haven't I told you many times that on the holy day you must do no work? When I am called by the Judge at the last day to give an account of the people committed to my care, what can I say of you?'

''Deed, Mr Randie,' replied the woman calmly, 'if ye dinna ken what tae answer, ye can just say till Him that he should hae sent the meal sooner!'

The Minister left.

Ballad Tales

Leezie Lindsay

Leezie was in a quandary. She didn't know what to do. A young stranger had come into her life and was pressing her to marry him. He was good looking and every time he came near her he put her head in a spin. There was just one snag. Judging by his clothes he was quite poor. If she wed him what might she be letting herself in for?

All she knew about him was that he came from the Highlands. That was all he had told her and in those days young ladies were not encouraged to ask too many questions.

'Will ye come wi me?' he whispered again and again. 'Will ye come to the Highlands and be my bride?'

She longed to say yes, but caution and a kind of dread held her back.

Leezie's real name was Elizabeth and she was the daughter of Sir Alexander and Lady Lindsay of Evelick Castle. She was used to a soft bed at night and the best of everything. She had never had to rough it. So while her heart told her that her wooer would make a wonderful husband, her head said, 'Beware! You'll regret it!'

If she went with the young stranger there was no saying where she might end up. The thought of it made her shiver.

There were no such doubts in her parents' minds. They liked him and approved. Her mother had told him, 'If I was in Leezie's place I'd marry you!' Leezie's younger sister Helen sighed and said, 'If I was old enough I'd wed you!' Even her servant maid urged Leezie to accept and made eyes at the young man every time he came to the door.

In the end Leezie's heart won. She said yes, packed her things and set off by his side, leaving Evelick and the friendly Sidlaws behind. For days they travelled through strange countryside. Often it was bleak and harsh and her spirits sank at the sight of it. What would lie at the end of this arduous journey? Although she hid it from him there were times when she regretted leaving her home so far behind.

One day he led her up a steep hill and halted at the top. 'Look,' he said. She gazed down on a green valley with well-tended pastures and woodlands. In the midst of it all stood a noble castle.

'You see that?' he said.

'Yes. What of it?'

'It all belongs to me and now it will be yours too.'

He pointed to the castle sitting in its fine gardens. 'There is your new home.'

She turned to him in astonishment. 'But—who are you then?'

33

'My name is Lord Ronald MacDonald.'

She wondered if she was dreaming as he told her he was the Chief of the Clan.

'But—why did you not tell me before?'

'Because I wanted you to trust me and to marry me for myself and not for what I am.'

He clasped her in his arms in a long embrace which she returned with all her heart. Then together they descended the hillside into the glen where the loyal clansmen were waiting to welcome him home and to greet his bride.

Leezie was never to regret her decision to risk all and go with her mysterious suitor. They were a perfect love match, living happily in their Highland home for the rest of their lives. Her sister Helen also married a Highland chief, the chief of Clan Macgregor. Her grand-daughter became the wife of the famous Rob Roy.

Leezie's story is celebrated in an old ballad, a version of which appears on p.146.

In Hot Water!

When Margaret Carnegie married John, Lord Gray, in 1741, she did not come empty-handed. She was the mistress of the great house of Kinfauns to which he now moved. Later he almost certainly would have lost it all and made them both homeless had it not been for his wife's quick presence of mind.

The '45 Uprising had erupted, Prince Charles had led his Army south and was now on his long road back into the Highlands. The Duke of Cumberland was in pursuit. When he reached Dundee, supporters of the House of Hanover went to pledge their support.

John Gray was Lord-Lieutenant of Forfarshire, and as such he went to convey official greetings and loyalty on behalf of the county. Perhaps becoming Laird of Kinfauns and Lord Lieutenant had inflated his opinion of his own importance. Or maybe he just had not heard of Cumberland's reputation for rudeness, especially to Scots who, as a nation, he detested.

At any rate John Gray considered the Duke's manner towards him was offhand and disgraceful and he set off home in a towering temper. So angry was he that, as he whipped on his horse, he resolved to leave first thing next morning and join the other side, Charles and the Jacobites.

When he went stamping into Kinfauns and told Margaret she was shocked and dismayed but, seeing the mood he was in, she knew better than to try to argue with her husband. Instead, she quietly suggested that, after his long ride, he should have his feet washed. 'I will do it for you,' she said.

Rather touched, he agreed and sat down while Margaret fetched a basin, told him to put his feet in it, and went to fetch hot water.

She boiled a kettle, carried it in to the room and then, as if by accident, poured it over her husband's feet.

His roars could be heard a long distance away and he spent a most uncomfortable night. In the morning there was no chance of him leaving his room, never mind travelling north.

He had the best possible nurse in his wife Margaret, but even so, it was weeks before he was fit to ride again. By that time the Jacobites had been defeated at Culloden, Prince Charles was a fugitive and the Uprising was over.

John Gray may never have admitted it, even to himself, but his wife had saved them both from calamity. He might well have died on Culloden Moor. If he had survived that awful battle he would have been heavily punished for taking part and, in all probability, Kinfauns would have been taken from him.

Lady Nairne, the song-writer, wrote amusing verses about this incident. In 'Ye'll Mount, Gudeman' (p.140) she changes the story of the 'accident' a little, though the outcome is the same.

From what one can tell of Lord Gray's character, somehow I don't think he would have been very pleased to know that he was the butt of Lady Nairne's humour in a comic song that at one time had all Perthshire laughing.

Sir James the Rose

Sir James was a hunted man. He had fought with a knight and killed him. Now the dead man's friends were seeking him. Led by Sir John Graeme they were determined to capture him and avenge the knight's death.

Accompanied only by a faithful servant, Donald, James turned his horse towards the Sidlaws and Auchterhouse where lived the one he loved, Matilda, daughter of the Earl of Buchan.

It was night when he tapped on her window. Quickly he told her of the danger he was in. She urged him to take a room for the night at a nearby inn.

He shook his head. There was a hidden bank not far away, above the mill near Lundie Crags. The grass was always long and deep. No one would guess he was there.

'I will come to you at daybreak,' she promised, 'and we will decide what's to be done.'

He kissed her and set off, making his secret way along by the Crags till he came to the grassy bank. There, exhausted, he and Donald wrapped themselves in their plaids and lay down for the night.

Meantime, at Auchterhouse, Matilda was answering a hammering at the door. Clustered outside was over a score of horsemen. At their head was Sir John Graeme.

'Have you seen Sir James the Rose?' he demanded. 'He has killed a gallant knight and we have been sent out to take him.'

At first Matilda lied.

'He passed by here on Monday,' she said. 'He'll be far away by now.'

The riders turned to go, but as they started off she suddenly called to them, 'Promise me a good reward and I'll tell you where to find him.'

Sir John Graeme rode back to her and bent down close. 'If we capture him,' he said, 'you shall have his purse.'

'There's a bank above the mill at Lundie,' she told him. 'You will find him there.'

James was in a deep sleep when they came on him. Donald lay nearby. Some of the men were for killing James where he lay but Graeme stopped them: 'Let it never be said we slew a sleeping man.'

He made them wait until James awoke. When he opened his eyes the first thing he saw was the faces looking down at him. He reached for his sword but it and his targe had gone.

He asked Graeme to spare his life, but Graeme refused. 'You showed no mercy to our friend and we will show none to you.'

Sir James turned to his servant. 'When I am dead, take my purse. It's full of gold and it's yours if you will carry my body home.'

The faithful Donald nodded, his eyes full of tears.

They slew James then, cut out his heart and carried it on the point of a spear to Auchterhouse.

'We are sorry,' said Graeme to Matilda. 'We could not bring you his purse. Instead, you may have his heart.'

The grisly sight was too much for Matilda. When she realised what she had done she broke down and wept bitterly. It is said that she wandered off into the Sidlaws, screaming, and was never seen again.

The above is the story of the tragedy as it is told in an old version of the ballad 'Sir James The Rose'. A later version makes a heroine of Matilda. She does not betray her lover and when he is killed in an underhand way by Sir John Graeme she draws the sword from James's side and falls on it herself. This whitewash version has not the same ring of truth as the earlier one (see p.132).

Telling the story in *Historic Scenes In Forfarshire* in 1875, William Marshall places the killing of James and Matilda's suicide in the grounds of the house of Auchterhouse. He claims that a large hawthorn tree near the house marked the spot where they fell. He rightly points out that other places have claimed to be the scene of the tragedy but adds, 'the claim of Auchterhouse appears to be as good as that of any of them'.

The ballad, he concludes, 'should be familiar to the dwellers of Auchterhouse age after age, and the Sidlaws should respond to its tender, plaintive strain'.

With that I agree.

Grey-Steil

Archibald Douglas was homesick. The soft English air was no substitute for the brisk winds of the Sidlaws, the flat landscape no match for the Braes of the Carse.

Alas, the Douglases were forbidden to set foot in Scotland and his beloved Kilspindie Castle had been given to another.

The Douglases, always plotters, forever seeking power and influence, had gone too far and, since 1528, James V had banished them into exile.

Yet there had been a time when the young James and the older man, Archibald

Douglas, had been close. The boy-king had recognised Archibald's qualities and trusted him. He called him 'Grey-steil' after his favourite character in a book he had enjoyed.

It had been a sad day for both men when Archibald Douglas had been forced into exile. But James knew there could be no exceptions. His nobles would insist on that. All leading members of the widespread Douglas family must leave.

Now Douglas felt he could stay away from Scotland no longer. He had to go back.

A few days later he slipped over the Border. There was no use making for Kilspindie: it was no longer his. He had no idea where he was to go but as he approached Stirling he heard that the King was there, at the Castle.

Dare he go to him, throw himself on his mercy? He knew it was a terrible risk, but he decided to take it.

James and his companions had been out hunting and were riding back to Stirling Castle when they saw the figure waiting ahead. The King stared, astonished.

'Yonder is my Grey-steil, Archibald of Kilspindie—if he be alive!' he exclaimed.

'It cannot be him, sire,' said one of his courtiers. 'No Douglas would dare come into your presence.'

However, when they rode closer they saw that it was indeed the Laird of Kilspindie.

Douglas had been a proud man but now he sank to his knees and pleaded to be forgiven. 'Only grant me a pardon,' he said, 'and I will meddle no more with public affairs.' He promised to live quietly and peaceably.

James did not as much as glance at him. His mind was in turmoil as he remembered what a good friend Archibald had been. But his nobles were watching him. Their hatred of the Douglases went very deep. They had always been jealous of the family's power and had rejoiced when they were banished.

James turned his face towards Stirling and spurred on his horse. His companions, relieved, followed closely.

Douglas hurried after them, calling to James, begging for forgiveness. He followed them all the way up the hill to the Castle. By the time he got there the Royal party was inside. Exhausted, he sank down on a stone by the gate. He was hot, out of breath, thirsty. There were servants about and he asked them if they would fetch him a glass of water. They knew who he was and refused, afraid they would be punished if they answered his request. Never had he felt so alone, so much of an outcast.

Inside the Castle, word of what was happening at the gate was brought to James and his eyes filled with tears. That his old friend should be treated in such a way… He lashed his servants with his tongue and ordered them to give Douglas the water he craved. Then he sent him a message.

He could not allow him to stay in Scotland. His vow to exile the Douglases had to stand. Instead, he promised to give him a safe escort to Leith and from there a passage to France.

Grey-steil accepted the offer sadly but gratefully. He went to France and lived there till he died, but later his son and heir, also Archibald, had the family lands restored to him and he returned to the Carse and Kilspindie (see p.136).

Fair Ellen

Before Tay Street in Perth was built, old houses clustered along the riverbank. In one of these lived a young tradesman, William Herdman, whose window looked over to the gardens and estates on the slopes of Kinnoull Hill.

One day, walking across the bridge, William's eye was caught by a beautiful face and a head of glorious brown hair. The girl did not notice him but he looked back at her flowing hair as she disappeared in the crowd.

Who was she? Would he ever see her again?

He did! Not many days later he passed her once more and this time he caught her eye and held it for a brief, blissful second before she looked away and hurried on.

After that, every time he crossed the bridge he watched for her in an agony of expectation. Came the day he dared to smile to her and—his heart leaped—she smiled back.

From that they started to exchange a greeting as they passed and, at last, as young people do, they found an excuse to stop and chat.

She told him her name was Ellen Rankine and that her father was a gardener at Bellwood which William could see from his window. You can imagine how, at nights, he gazed across the river. He could not see Ellen but just to imagine her was enough.

Soon they were meeting by arrangement and she took him home to meet her father and mother. Before long the two lovers were engaged to be married.

It was then it happened. A quarrel sprang up between William and Mr Rankine. It was a trivial matter but both lost their temper and bitter words were exchanged.

Perhaps if William had apologised the quarrel could have been settled, but he was too proud to do that. Instead, determined to shake the dust of Perth from his feet he sought out a recruiting officer and enlisted in the Army.

He was sent to Spain where French forces had invaded the Iberian Peninsula. Britain was attempting to drive them out, with the support of Spanish and Portuguese troops.

The British suffered a setback and retreated to Corunna on a long and terrible trek in the winter of 1809. Under their leader, Sir John Moore, they dug in at Corunna.

On 16 January the French attacked. There was no stopping them. Sir John Moore was killed in the battle and so was the young soldier, William Herdman.

The news of William's death had a devastating effect on Ellen. In no time at all, William would hardly have recognised the pale, listless girl who now shrank from the world.

Her parents did all they could to reason with her and console her but it was no use. She took to walking about in the Sidlaws and through the countryside as if searching for someone or something. She would be seen hurrying along, bare-footed, waving a red handkerchief in her right hand. With her left she held up, in an untidy bundle, the once beautiful brown hair which had first attracted William when he saw her on the bridge.

The country people, who met her on the hills, or along the tracks, were full of pity for the distracted creature. They tried to help her by offering food and shelter. Today she would have been taken into care but then anyone like Ellen, deranged in mind, was allowed to wander at will, sleeping under hedges or in cold barns, until they died a merciful death.

One man who had known Ellen by sight before her breakdown was Andrew Sharpe who lived at Bridgend. He was a shoemaker to trade but he was also a poet, painter and musician. Remembering the lovely girl she had been he was deeply saddened at the change that had come over her.

Haunted by the tragedy he sat down and wrote a poem about her. In 'Corunna's Lone Shore' he imagines Ellen lamenting her loss as she wanders alone. This is the last verse:

> And here as I travel all tattered and torn,
> By bramble and briar, over mountain and moor,
> Ne'er a bird bounds aloft to salute the new morn
> But warbles aloud, 'Oh! Corunna's lone shore.'
> It is heard in the blast when the tempest is blowing,
> It is heard in the white broken waterfall flowing,
> It is heard in the songs of the reaping and mowing,
> Oh, my poor bleeding heart! Oh, Corunna's lone shore!

This song (see p.152) used to be very popular in Perthshire and never failed to bring a tear to the eye of those who remembered the fate of Fair Ellen Rankine.

Meg o' Liff

The village of Liff lies off the busy A923, not far from Muirhead and Dundee's pleasure park, Camperdown, but out of sight of them.

Here, if a ballad is to be believed, there once lived a couple, John Rough and his wife Meg.

John was a weaver, a hard enough life I'm sure, but it was made harder by Meg who, since the day they were married, had nagged and scolded him. Poor John got little peace for she raged at him from morning to night, never pleased with anything he did.

For forty years John had been working on a web, a huge piece of cloth on his loom. Now it was almost completed. The day before Christmas he rose early and sat down to work as usual. All day he toiled without stopping and when the sun sank and darkness crept over the cottage he was at last finished.

He rose from his seat with a sigh. 'God be thankit,' he said as he slipped off his apron, stretched himself and sat down by the kitchen fire.

But he had only just lit his pipe and was beginning to enjoy it when Meg appeared in front of him, her face twisted with temper, demanding to know why he was sitting there and calling him a 'lazy snool' and worse. 'Get back to your loom!' she ranted.

In vain he pleaded that he had finished the web and deserved a rest. 'It's Christmas nicht,' he reminded her. 'Surely for aince ye'll be at peace wi' me.'

There was no pacifying her. When he didn't rise obediently to his feet she gave him a mighty slap with her open hand. His pipe, the best friend he had, flew from his mouth and smashed in the fireplace.

Still he sat there, suffering in his usual silence while her strident voice rose higher and higher.

But suddenly, on the stroke of ten, another sound was heard—a knock on the door. It flew open and in rushed a crowd of hideous old hags, yelling and screaming. They made straight for Meg and surrounded her. Some seized her arms, some her legs, others her shoulders. One stuffed her mouth with brimstone to choke her cries.

As quickly as they had come the hags left, pouring out through the door with Meg a captive in their midst. She was helpless in their terrible grasp as they flew through the darkness, not stopping till they came to the hill of Hurly Hawkin.

There they flung her down on the top and then danced and sang in a circle round her, a dreadful sight and noise under the night sky.

This is what they sang:

> 'We've got her noo,
> What shall we do?
> Sisters say!
>
> We've got her noo
> On Hurly Hawkin,
> What shall we do?
> Skelp her! Skelp her!
> Nane will help her,
> Skelp her bare
> For temper brackin'.
>
> Bring the chair,
> Sit her there,
> We will cure her
> Randy talkin',
> This we'll do
> On Hurly Hawkin!'

As they chanted and danced a black chair rose from the ground. The hags dragged Meg over to it, stripped off most of her clothes and pushed her on the chair.

Now each of the creatures reached deep into her ragged garments and pulled out a tawse, a leather-thonged strap. They started to whack her with these as hard as they could and because there was no back to the chair she had no protection from the blows.

Poor Meg. She could not escape the awful pain as her raw skin turned black and blue. She could not scream—her voice just would not come out.

We've got her noo
On Hurly Hawkin,
What shall we do?
Skelp her! Skelp her!

But something was happening in her heart. From feeling sorry for herself she suddenly thought of her husband and the suffering she had inflicted on him down the years.

She had never felt pity before but she felt it now, pity and regret that she had made his life such a misery. Words came to her lips at last. 'John, forgi'e me!' she murmured. Tears, the first she had ever shed, flowed down her cheeks.

In an instant the hags stood still. They put away the leather straps. They lifted Meg off the chair and, with surprising gentleness, dressed her again. Then, laughing now and shouting with glee, they carried her back to Liff.

As 12 o'clock rang out on the kirk bell an exhausted John was lying in bed asleep. He did not hear the chimes welcome Christmas morning nor did he hear the hags sweep into the room and lay his wife by his side.

Their job done the hags left the house and wound their way down the Den o' Gray.

In the morning, when John awoke and looked at Meg's face, he knew at once that she had changed. Gone was the ill temper, the seething rage. And from that day on no man could have wished for a sweeter and more loving wife.

John never asked her where she had been or what had happened so he never knew what she had gone through up there on the hill of Hurly Hawkin. It was enough for him that she was always kind and gentle and would sit at nights smiling over at him with love in her eyes as he smoked his pipe contentedly by the ingle neuk (see p.146).

On the Lighter Side

The Bad Word

The farmer at Pitroddie was working at the harvest one day when he was heard to utter a bad word. Since he was an elder of Errol church this lapse caused a lot of talk. It reached the ears of his kirk session, who were very shocked indeed and issued him with a rebuke. Possibly thinking they were a bunch of hypocrites the farmer refused to accept it.

The matter divided families up and down the Carse. His friends thought the session had no right to reprimand him while his detractors felt he deserved it.

In the end he and his supporters applied for a church to be opened at Pitroddie. A minister was found and he and his friends left Errol church and formed a new congregation. All because of one unfortunate word on the harvest field.

Macduff of St Madoes

When the Rev. J.R. Macduff moved from the church at Kettins to St Madoes on the other side of the Sidlaws he was delighted. The only drawback he saw was the small size of the parish. It was only a mile square.

'I fancy,' he said to William, his beadle, 'I shall be able to visit the entire parish in six weeks.'

'Sax weeks!' said the astonished William. 'A wee moment some efternin!'

With Lord Kinnaird and others, Macduff worked hard to improve the standard of housing for farm labourers and fishermen in the Carse. He tried to improve their minds too. He wrote *A Tract for Bothy Lads* and helped to run evening classes and a lending library.

These efforts were not always appreciated. One man, being urged to use the library, retorted, 'We are no hired to work your work *and* read your books tae!'

Work Suspended

In his book *The Evangel In Gowrie* (1911) the Rev. Adam Philip describes his childhood memories of a Sabbath on the Braes of the Carse in the first half of the nineteenth century.

He recalls seeing a dignified elder enter the kirk in his Sunday suit, with one boot highly polished and the other 'covered with glaur'.

The farmer, he explains, had returned so late from market the night before that his servant lass had time to clean only one of his boots before the clock struck midnight and all work had to cease.

Serpents, Fairies, Brownies and the Deil Himsel

The Nine Maidens

Nine maidens were they, spotless, fair,
With silver skins, bright golden hair,
Blue-eyed, vermilion-cheeked, nowhere
Their match in Glen of Ogilvy.

James Cargill Guthrie.

The poem was written just over a century ago but the legend is very old. How old it is impossible to say. All I know is that it has made the little Glen Ogilvy a very special place. I am sure I am not the only person who has felt an air of holiness on its peaceful braes.

The tradition is that a saint lived here, Donevald or Donevaldus by name, in the eighth century. The nine maidens were his daughters. Their mother? There seems to be no record of her.

The girls all lived together and, being raised by a saint, led simple, blameless lives. They also worked hard, farming the land and rearing livestock. It was said that they ate only once a day and then just barley bread and water.

One of the girls, Mazota, had strange powers over animals. As long as she was there the wild goats did not nibble a blade of their crops.

As they grew older the sisters helped their father with his missionary work. Like him they went out on journeys across Scotland spreading the Word.

They must have won high esteem and much love, for when old Donevald died, the King of the Picts offered the 'virgin-dochters' a home, a chapel and some land at Abernethy in Fife where the Celtic monastery was linked with one of the great women of the early church, St Bridget.

There the sisters continued their good works into their old age. As they passed away one by one, they were buried under a great oak tree. A shrine was built to commemorate them and was a place of pilgrimage until the Reformation.

And to their grave from every land
Came many a sorrowing pilgrim band,
The oak to kiss whose branches grand
Waved o'er the maids of Ogilvy.

Some of their names linger on. Fincana was later shortened to St Fink and there was a chapel dedicated to her on the north side of Strathmore looking across the wide valley to the Sidlaws. Fyndocha is remembered in the ruins of a chapel on the island of Inishail, Loch Awe. Findo Gask, near Perth, is believed to be named after her. Mazota gave her name, abbreviated, to St Maik and to a well at Drumoak, Aberdeen. The names of some of the other sisters may lie hidden in place-names for which we now have no explanation.

These good women were long remembered in and around Glen Ogilvy and Glamis nearby. Their lives and works were annually celebrated on 15 June. As late as the seventeenth century the Kirk Session of Glamis forbade local girls from going on a pilgrimage to Abernethy on that date.

> Nine maidens fair in life were they,
> Nine maidens fair in death's last fray,
> Nine maidens fair in fame alway,
> The maids of Glen of Ogilvy.

The Maids of Strathmartine

On the other side of the Sidlaws from Glen Ogilvy lies Strathmartine. At first thought the two places would seem worlds apart, the tiny glen in the Angus country-side and the strath on the very edge of Dundee. In fact, a crow flying in a straight line from one to the other would cover the distance in minutes. Only Craigowl, Auchterhouse Hill and their neighbours separate them.

The strange thing is that Strathmartine, too, has its tale of nine maidens. They were the daughters of a farmer at Pitempton, and he sent one of them to fetch water from the well. When she didn't return he sent another to find out what had happened. She didn't come back either so he sent the next one, and so on until all nine had gone to the well and not returned.

'That's strange', he thought. 'I must go and see what's keeping them.'

He went to the well and was horrified to find all his daughters lying dead. Curled around them were two huge snakes. They were about to attack the farmer but he ran off and escaped.

He roused everyone in Strathmartine and they hurried to the scene and stared at the snakes from a safe distance.

Then a young man called Martin stepped forward. He had been betrothed to one of the daughters and now he drew his sword and closed in on them.

The snakes reared and lunged at him but he did not flinch. His sword flashed in the sunlight, once, twice. Both snakes were badly wounded. They started to crawl away and Martin followed. Taking his lead, the bolder amongst the crowd went too, arming themselves with sticks and stones.

The snakes were making for the hills where they would no doubt have crawled into holes in the rocks, but Martin caught up with them at Balluderon and killed them.

Martin's Stone stands in a field on Balkello Farm. This is an early sculptured stone on which are carved two horsemen, a snake or serpent, a Pictish beast and a two-rod symbol.

In Dundee Museum (McManus Galleries) can be seen another Pictish stone. When I first saw this one in the 1950s it was standing in a garden in Strathmartine, and I recall my excitement when I spotted it, went into the garden and traced the two intertwined snakes with my fingers. The snakes of the story? Who knows.

The garden had at one time belonged to the Strathmartine schoolmaster but by the time I saw it, the house was in other hands. In the 1960s the stone was brought into the museum where it is one of the small and valuable collection of Pictish stones.

Another version of the story has it that it was a dragon that Martin slew. The name Strathmartine, it claims, comes from the shouts of the crowd as he caught up with the creature, 'Strike, Martin!'

Baldragon, in the strath, according to this version, is where the killing took place and this old rhyme records the event:

> It was tempit at Pitempton,
> Draggelt at Ba'dragon,
> Stricken at Strike-Martine,
> And killed at Martin Stane.

There may well have been other sculptured stones in Strathmartine. One is recorded as having been found in the gable of an old house demolished in 1824. On it was the figure of a man carrying a weapon. The strange thing about this figure was that he had the head of a hog.

The Nine Maidens Well, where the girls met their fate, was on the south bank of the Dighty Burn, opposite the old kirkyard.

It is not surprising that the district has these old tales and beliefs since human habitation in Strathmartine goes back at least to Pictish times as the stones and the name Pitempton tell us (place-names beginning with Pit are Pictish in origin). You can get close to the Picts by visiting the fine early souterrain at Tealing. There were three others, maybe more, in the parish.

The poignant tale of the Nine Maidens will have been told in Strathmartine long before the city of Dundee came anywhere close to its boundaries.

The Green Serpent

More than one wife was stolen from Kilspindie Castle by the fairies. In the story 'The Kilspindie Ghost' (see p.123) the Laird was not greatly concerned by the loss of his wife. The second Laird was very different: he loved his wife dearly and longed to have her back. Yet when the chance came, he failed to take it.

He was sitting one night brooding on his loneliness when a green serpent came gliding into the room. It was so hideous that he shrank away from it, even when it told him it was his wife and that this was what the fairies had done to her.

It said that it had managed to slip away from them when they were not looking.

This was the only chance she would ever get to return to human form. All he had to do to break the terrible spell was make the sign of the cross. She would then change back into his wife again.

The serpent stared up at the Laird, waiting, but he was so horrified at the sight of the creature he was unable to speak or move.

He watched, helpless, as the serpent turned and slithered from the room uttering these words as it went:

> 'Weirdless Kilspindie,
>   Weirdless shall ye be;
> Weirdless Kilspindie,
>   Till the day ye dee.'

'Weirdless' is Scots for unfortunate and so the poor man was, for he never saw the serpent or his wife again and was dogged by ill luck for the rest of his days.

The Stolen Wife

The Laird of Balmachie went one day on business to Dundee, leaving his wife ill in bed. Balmachie lies south of Carnoustie, and when he returned at gloaming he rode past Carlungie with its souterrain.

He was winding his way between some green knolls and hummocks when he was amazed to see, crossing in front of him, a troop of fairies carrying a litter. In the fading light he could see there was a figure on it so he rode over, drew his sword and laid it across the litter, calling, 'In the name of God, release your captive!'

The fairies at once dropped the litter and disappeared. All was still. The Laird got down from his horse and bent over the litter. To his astonishment he found the person lying in it was his wife still in her bedclothes.

He wrapped her in his coat, sat her on his horse in front of him and rode home. When he got there he took her, not to her own room but to another in a different part of the house, where he left her in the care of a friend.

He then went to the room where he had left his wife that morning. There she was, lying in bed, and whenever she saw him she started complaining of how ill she felt and how badly she had been neglected while he was away.

The Laird pretended great sympathy for her. He said she must get out of bed so that it could be remade.

'But I can't get out of bed!' she wailed. 'I'm far too weak.'

The Laird said not to worry, he would carry her. He bent over and took her up in his arms and pretended to be going towards a chair. Then he turned to the fireplace and threw her with all his force into the flames.

She didn't burn. Instead she bounced from the fire and shot straight up through the roof, leaving a great hole in the slates.

Much relieved, the Laird went back to his real wife and told her what had happened. She said that, just as dusk was falling a host of wee folk had swarmed in at the window like bees. They had lifted her from the bed and carried her out through the window after which she remembered nothing until she saw her husband standing over her under the evening sky.

The hole in the roof by which the fairy imposter had escaped was repaired, but every year after that a storm of wind would rise and open it up again at exactly the same place.

The Magic Words

At the other end of the Sidlaws from where Balmachie's wife was taken by the fairies, there is a story of another kidnap attempt.

Lord Kinnaird was riding home late one night when he heard voices carried on the wind. It was the fairies and they were singing:

'Mak it neat and mak it sma',
Like the lady o' the Ha';
Mak it neat and mak it tidy,
Just like Lord Kinnaird's lady.'

He galloped home, leapt from his horse and rushed into the castle and up to his wife's room. A terrible sight met his eyes: a horde of fairies was gathered round the bed and were dragging her from it. He pushed his way through them and held her fast while striking out at the fairies with his riding-whip.

Fortunately he knew some magic words that could break their power. He spoke them now and instantly they all fled, scrambling out of the window as fast as they could go.

On the bed beside Lady Kinnaird lay a wooden figure or 'stock' which they had dressed up and intended to leave in her place. She was none the worse but it had been a narrow escape.

They Used to Say...

At one time the belief in fairies was strong all along the Sidlaws. One of the places they were thought to live was Kinpurnie Hill. *Our Meigle Book* records an old belief that fairy men from the Sidlaws would steal newborn babies and young girls and 'carry them off to their caverns or underground houses'. In the 1870s the author of *Meigle, Past And Present* wrote, 'It is said that men in this district have cohabited with females of the fairy race.'

Dunsinnan and the Black Hill area was one of their abodes. According to Melville in *The Fair Land of Gowrie*, 'on summer nights they descended to the meadows, where they danced at a spot called "Fairygreen".'

In the Carse a man called Robbie Curr told yarns of the fairies from his own

experience. He was born at Trotack Mill and later lived at Rait where he enter-
tained his neighbours with his stories. Here he is, talking to a young friend, Will:

'When bidin at the Mill o'Trotack, a young chield like yoursel, when I would
hae been comin hame frae seein the lasses late at nicht, I wad hae heard the mill
gaun at a braw canny sheugh, and I lookit in at the keyhole an seen them a' thrang
in the meal trough.'

'What like were they?' asked Will.

'Little creatures wi green goonies an bits o' din [darker hues] and yellow caps
on their heids.'

He told how they once invaded the family home in the middle of the night and
were dancing on the floor to a piper perched on the plate rack.

The noise was terrible and his father sat up in bed and ordered them out. When
they didn't go, he jumped out and chased them up the chimney, firing a shot after
them. Next morning his young mare took one drink of water and fell down dead,
the cow turned sick and died and the hens choked on their food.

An old woman, Mrs Donaldson of the Brodlie, fared better from a fairy visit.
She woke up at night and heard them working her spinning wheel. Impressed by
the amount they could do in a short time she rose and gripped the rim of the wheel
asking them to leave her some of their speed. Every night after that, said Robbie,
'she span a hasp o' yarn in the time the maid was puttin on the pot wi the sowans.'

Robbie had tales of changelings, the fairy babies that would be left when they
stole human children. His aunt had a lovely thriving bairn. It was, he said, 'the
picture o' its faither'.

At about two months old it changed. It wouldn't eat and never stopped crying.
It would give everyone 'as auld-farrant a look as a man o' eighty.'

Fortunately the woman knew how to get rid of the creature. She built up a
huge fire and sat it in a chair close up in front of it. Then she repeated this rhyme:

'If ye be my son Tam,
Fire shall not ye scan;
If ye frae fairies come,
Flee ye up the lum!'

'It sat a while, till, wi the heat o' the fire, its face was as red as a north-west
moon. Then it rose a wee abune the chair, an at last it flew up the lum!'

It would hardly have reached the top of the chimney when Robbie's aunt
heard a crying sound behind her. She turned and saw her own baby lying safe and
sound on the floor.

Sometimes the fairies would steal a child and give it to another family as a
present. Charlie Grant was a farmer at the Quilky. One night he heard a noise from
the kiln where he dried his corn. As he approached he was aware of a sound
overhead like wild geese. Then he heard a baby crying.

He called his wife Jenny to bring a light and when she did so there was 'a bonny
bairn about twa years auld sittin in the kiln'.

They already had children of their own but in any case they knew the infant
had been stolen from somebody else. They asked all around and found that it

belonged to a mother in Saucher in Strathmore. One moment it had been playing at the cottage door and the next it had disappeared. The Grants returned the child to her none the worse of its experience. In fact it had benefited from its time away, for the fairies had taught it to spin and it could do so faster and better than anyone else.

Water Kelpies

These were horses that lived in lochs and rivers. A famous one lived in the Boat Hole, the deep pool on the Isla where the river is now crossed by Crathie Bridge. The Dean joins the Isla close to this point and the kelpie used to rush along one river and up the other, swelling the water and causing such a commotion that it terrified all who saw it. He seemed to love it best when the rivers were in spate and he would tumble and wallow in the flood.

The kelpie got the blame when, one stormy night, the ferry boat at Crathie was overturned and a woman, two men and a horse were drowned.

Since the bridge was built in 1819 there do not seem to have been any sightings of this malevolent creature. Perhaps he objected to the bridge, or did he end his days as a work horse on Balmyre farm?

The farmer is said to have captured him, put him in harness and forced him to work. An old rhyme records the kelpie's unhappiness:

> Sair back and sair banes,
> Carryin' auld Balmyre's stanes.

A similar rhyme is recorded from the North Esk:

> Sair back and sair banes,
> Carryin' the Laird o' Murphy's stanes.

Here the kelpie had been made to carry the stones for the building of the Castle of Murphy:

> When Murphy's Laird his biggin reared,
> I carryt a' the stanes,
> And mony a chiel has heard me squeal,
> For sair birzed back and banes.

The kelpie never forgave the Laird:

> The Laird o' Murphy will never thrive,
> So long as Kelpie is alive.

The North Esk and the Kerbet Water were both well known to be the abode of kelpies.

The lurking dangers of the Dean are recognised in this rhyme:

> The dowie Dean it rins its lane,
> And ilka seven year it taks ane.

Robbie Curr told how, one fine Monday morning, he was working in the Mill of Errol grinding oats for the Laird o' Murie. When he noticed that the water was not flowing properly he went out to see what was the matter and found a kelpie in the lade. He said it had long hair like seaweed and wore a kind of cloak.

The cloak had a tear in it which it was intent on mending. It had a piece of cloth which it laid on the hole, trying it this way and that and saying, 'No, it'll no do this way… No, it'll no do that way… No, it'll no do that way either.'

Robbie picked up a large stone and said, 'If it winna do that way, it'll no do *that* way!'

The beast was furious. It plunged under the water and then threw up its head and cried:

> 'Auld man Madison,
> This you shall rue,
> Some misty morning,
> I'll meet wi' you!'

Madison was the local dyker and the kelpie had evidently mistaken Robbie for him. The following Sunday was a very misty morning. Madison went for a walk along the side of the stream and was never seen again. Robbie had no doubt the kelpie had got him.

The Tay Mermaid

Robbie also told a story of a mermaid, though he did not claim to have seen her himself. He said the creature lived in the Tay and used to come ashore near Daleally to comb her long golden hair. The locals left her alone but then a stranger came into the district, Jock Jouthers. He decided he would catch her.

He watched her and saw that she often sat underneath a certain tree near the shore. He took a rope and tied it to the tree, coiling it up at the foot. The other end he fastened round his waist. Then he hid and waited.

As usual the mermaid swam ashore and sat under the tree. When she had been combing her hair for some time Jock pulled the rope and the coils slipped firmly round her. He ran forward and tightened it, making her prisoner. She pleaded with him to let her go but he wouldn't listen. He carried her off to the nearest house.

The following day was Sunday and everybody went off to church except a young servant lass called May who was left to make the kail and rock the cradle. She had been instructed to make sure the mermaid did not escape.

The mermaid, still tied with rope, watched May as she stirred the kail on the fire. May was enchanted when the lovely creature broke into a sweet, soothing song:

> 'Skim the kail,
> Bonny May,
> Skim aye the kail.'

May did not notice that, as she was stirring, the mermaid was loosening her knots one by one. When she had loosened the last one, she slipped free and was out of the house in an instant and making straight for the shore.

As she swam through the water she was heard singing another song:

'Never, never mair
Will I kame my yellow hair
On the bonny flowery banks
O' the Tay.'

She was never seen again.

Witches

'Cow's milk and mare's milk,
And every beast that bears milk,
Between St Johnstone's and Dundee,
Come a' to me, come a' to me!'

By saying this verse while tugging at a hair-rope in the rhythm of milking, a witch could draw milk from every cow between Perth and Dundee. The rope would be made up of tufts of hair taken from cows' tails and it would have a knot for each cow.

To protect their cows, farmers would attach to their tails sprigs of rowan tied with red thread.

Strathmore farmers believed that the butter made from 'stolen' milk was always paler in colour.

In the latter part of the nineteenth century the assistant minister of Collace, the Rev. Andrew Bonar, was shocked to notice that it was common practice for the farmers to hang a horseshoe on the byre door to keep the witches out. He urged them to take the horseshoes down and was pleased to note, as he went around the farms, that many of them had gone. Then he discovered that the farmers had simply placed them inside the doors instead!

According to Robert Chambers in his *Popular Rhymes* some cows were aware when their milk was being taken by witchcraft and would low as if they were in pain. When the old folk heard this they knew at once what was happening.

Some farmers would protect their cattle when they were in the byre by taking a twig or branch of rowan, binding it with scarlet thread and laying it across the byre threshold. Another method was to find a four-leaved clover and fix it to the cow's stall.

If a cow was losing its milk to a witch, the farmer could find out who the witch was by putting a pair of his trousers over the beast's horns, one leg over each horn. When he turned the cow loose it would run straight to the door of the guilty party.

In Strathmore, witches were burned to death on a hillock between Kinloch and Cronan known as the Witches' Knowe.

One unfortunate woman was burned in a tar barrel at Drumkilbo House in

1704. She was a Nairne, a distant relative of Lady Nairne, the songwriter. Her only fault, it seems, was that she had come into possession of Drumkilbo and the heir, George Nairne, was impatient to inherit it.

Witches were also burned on the Law Knowe, Kinpurnie Hill. The last woman to die there was carried to the Knowe on a cart. Folk had come from far and near to watch. They were hurrying past the cart, keen to be early and get a good view of the proceedings.

As they went by the poor woman nodded and smiled to them and said to her keepers, 'What are they a' fleein' at? There can be nothing dune till I gang!'

When the cart neared the Knowe, people were still streaming up the slope. She sat down calmly, took out her knitting from a large pocket and said, 'I'll just sew a thread till the people a' gaither.'

She went to her death just as calmly.

A woman called Girzie Jamphrey was tried for witchcraft, found guilty and condemned to be burned at the stake in Dundee.

She was locked in a cell in the town prison and three men were put on guard to watch her and prevent her from sleeping. They kept her awake for two days and two nights, but on the third night they dropped off to sleep for a short time.

When they awoke she was sprawled halfway up the cell wall. They pulled her down and she cried, 'Oh, ye micht hae let me be till I had gotten the sowans o' Ballumbie skinned!'

The men swore they saw the skin of the sowans on her hands.

Ever after there was only half a skin on the sowans made at Ballumbie.

In the parish of Auchterhouse there was at one time a well dedicated to the Virgin Mary. Its healing properties attracted so-called witches and charmers.

It has been forgotten how often folk resorted to charms. They were sought after for all sorts of purposes: to cure, to make someone fall in love, to protect or bring good fortune.

In 1652 a Mrs Robertson in Auchterhouse had a daughter who suffered from an eye trouble. The anxious mother went for help to a Janet Fyffe who taught her this charm:

> 'Fish beare fin and fulle beare gall,
> All ye ill of my bairn's eyen
> In ye will fall.'

Mrs Robertson took her child to the Kirkton Well, washed its eyes in the water and repeated the words. The minister found out about it and she was brought before the Kirk Session. She and Janet Fyffe were ordered to confess to the Presbytery. As punishment they had to sit in the church in sackcloth on the stool of repentance for several sabbaths.

When it was felt that they had done this long enough they were ordered to make public repentance in the church. Janet Fyffe did so, but poor Mrs Robertson could not appear: she had died.

Old Knap

A wild character known as Old Knap or the Deil o' the Carse was believed to have sold his soul to the Devil. He was much feared and there was considerable relief when he died. On the day of his funeral the snow was deep on the ground. The party carrying the coffin found the road blocked. Unable to take it any further they laid it down and left it. When they returned later the coffin was empty.

The Brownie o' Errol

There was once a brownie lived in hiding at the Mains o' Errol. It was before Robbie Curr moved to the Mill but he said he often heard the farm ploughmen talking about it. They described the brownie as just like a little man but covered with thick brown hair.

He was a helpful creature as brownies often were and used to thrash the corn at night when the men had gone home from the mill. Several men worked there but the brownie would do more in a night than they could manage in a month.

In payment the farmer's wife left him a cogful of brose or sowans every night. It doesn't sound much but brownies were not greedy creatures. All they wanted was to be left alone to get on with the work they set themselves. They liked to be in a routine and hated any departure from it or any interference with their habits. So long as their ways were respected and they got what they believed they deserved, all was well. But any breakdown in the system or any complaint and they were likely to fly into a rage and leave for good. They also took deep offence if given anything over and above what they expected.

Things first started to go wrong with the Mains o' Errol brownie when one night the mill workers were late going for their supper. The brownie had been waiting for them to leave so that he could come out of hiding and get his. He had grown hungry, so hungry that he supped the skin off their sowans.

When the men saw their sowans they didn't know who to blame and made a great to-do about it. The brownie overheard their complaints and was not pleased.

A few days later their helpings of sowans were smaller than usual. Again they grumbled and moaned. The brownie, watching them from a corner, snarled, 'You needna blame me, for I only got two slags and a harls.'

It was the farmer's wife who finally pushed the brownie too far. It was coming on winter and she thought he must be feeling the cold. She left him a little cloak and hood to keep him warm.

It was entirely the wrong thing to do. The brownie flew into a terrible rage at this unlooked for gift.

That night the farmer's wife heard him singing this song beneath her window:

> 'Ochone, I maun flit,
> I can do nae mair guid,

Since the guidwife has gien me
A cloak an a hood.

I can thrash here nae mair,
Sae I'll noo gang awa'
An tak up my quarters
In some ither ha'

Whaur I'll get brose substantial,
Whaur sowans will be rife,
Whaur there's nae greedy ploughmen,
Nor timid guidwife.

Whaur the first will ne'er grudge
A drap sowans for my wark,
Nor the last ever dress me
In cloak, coat or sark.

For noo I maun flit,
I can do nae mair guid
Since the guidwife has gien me
A cloak an a hood.'

True to his word he was never seen in the district again.

The Bird in the Bush

There was a minister at Collace who used to meet the Deil in his garden. He came every gloaming when the minister was in his garden taking a walk.

The minister's wife used to see them from the window, walking and talking together, and she wondered who this man might be and why her husband never invited him into the Manse.

One evening she hid in a bush to hear what they were talking about. Along the two of them came in deep conversation. As they drew near she heard the stranger say, 'Will ye no gie me the power over anything? Will ye no gie me the bird in the bush?'

'Not the meanest reptile,' answered her husband firmly. And then, 'Get ye behind me, Satan!'

She knew then who the stranger was and she crept fearfully back into the house.

Later, when her husband came in, she admitted what she had done and what she had overheard. The minister was shocked and upset. He pointed out to her the narrow escape she had had. 'If I had granted his request you would now be in the Deil's power.'

Davie and the Deil

Davie Oudney's mother was a witch. He knew that, for more than once he had come on a coven of them dancing on the green near his home at Balthayock, above Glen Carse. Watching from a distance he had recognised his mother among them. What was more she seemed to be the head one amongst them, the leader of the dance.

One day the Deil waylaid Davie and tried to persuade him to join the witches at their next gathering. Davie knew better than to argue with Auld Nick. He told him he would think about it.

The Deil was disappointed. He had Davie's mother in his power and he had thought it would be easy to get Davie as well. He didn't give up trying either. Every now and again he waited for Davie on the road and did his best to entice him. Davie always played for time and said he would consider it. 'Gie me time to think aboot it,' he would say, though he had no intention of ever saying yes.

The last time it happened was on a fine frosty night with snow on the ground. Davie was walking along the head of the brae at the Den o' Balthayock. He had been away collecting a new door that a neighbour had made for him and he was carrying it home on his back.

Suddenly there was Auld Nick standing in front of him. He demanded a final answer from Davie. He said he had waited long enough and his patience was at an end. Davie was not going another step until he had given him his decision.

Davie admitted afterwards that he had been frightened. 'I was feard to say no,' he said. 'He was sic an awfu like sicht. He must have been twelve or fifteen feet high wi a great gapin mou and lang teeth. His een were shinin like twa penny caundles.'

Davie tried to put him off as he had done before but it was no use. The Deil would not listen. So at last Davie came out with it: he would have nothing to do with him or the witches. 'That's my answer for you!' he shouted.

The Deil's eyes glowed even brighter than before and his face went black with rage.

Davie could not get past him but he suddenly thought of the door on his back. He flung it down in front of him, jumped on it and pushed off down the brae. Auld Nick had to leap out of the way or he would have got his shins broken.

Davie expected the door to stop at the bottom of the Den, but it was going so fast it shot right up the other side. Even there it did not stop but ran back down and up to where it had started. Off it sped again, down to the bottom, up the other side and back again, never for a moment losing speed. He tried to roll off but found he was stuck to is as if glued.

The Deil, watching from the top of the brae, shouted, 'Will ye join the squad noo, Davie?'

Davie never answered but clung to the door as it went up and down, up and down, for hour after hour.

At last the darkness of night began to lift and a faint red light coloured the sky.

Davie never answered but clung to the door as it went up and down...

Clear on the frosty air came the first cockcrow of morning from the bird at Tullyhoo. Auld Nick up on the brae gave a horrible laugh that thundered along the Den and next moment he vanished.

No sooner had he done so than the door stopped still. Davie crawled off it, got to his feet, lifted it up on his back and made his late way home.

He said the Deil never came after him again, but just in case he ever did Davie always carried a sprig of rowan close to his chest to ward him off.

The door, luckily, was none the worse of its adventures and Davie often looked at it and remembered the wild night he spent on it, the night he gave the Deil his answer.

On the Lighter Side

Plain Thinking

An Angus laird had no time for modern theories about the universe. 'Dinna tell me,' he said, 'that the earth's shaped like an orange and that it whirls roond aboot ilka twenty-four 'oors. It's a' nonsense! The Seidlaw Hills lie to the north and the Tay to the sooth when I gang to my bed at nicht. In the morning when I rise I find them the same. That's guid proof that the earth disna turn roond.

'I'll tell ye what it is—an' I speak wi' the authority of ane wha's gie'n the maitter a deal o' thocht—the earth's spread oot just like a muckle barley scone, in which the Howe o' Strathmore represents a knuckle mark.'

Two Gifts

The Rev. Dr Dow, minister of Errol, was great friends with the minister of Kilspindie, the Rev. Dr Duff. The latter loved snuff and one New Year's Day he received a well-filled snuff-box inscribed with these lines:

'Dr Dow to Dr Duff,
Snuff! Snuff! Snuff!'

Dr Dow's weakness was a glass of toddy (whisky and hot water) and his friend Duff replied with a beautiful hot-water jug on the lid of which were the words:

'Dr Duff to Dr Dow,
Fou! Fou! Fou!' (Full, drunk.)

Bright Boy

The wife of a Kilspindie ploughman was expecting a visit from the minister and had spent hours coaching her ten-year-old son so that he would give the correct answers to whatever he was asked.

Her conversation with the great man went well and then he turned to the boy. 'Now, lad, who made you?'

'God made me.'

'Quite correct, boy. And who redeemed you?'

'Christ redeemed me.'

'Very good. You're a clever fellow.' He put a hand on the boy's head. 'Who cut your hair?'

'The Holy Ghost, sir.'

Put Down

Principal Caird, Professor of Divinity at Glasgow, used to tell how, when he was minister of Errol, he found the church acoustics not very satisfactory. As the congregation was quite small he suggested to the beadle that they might board off one of the side aisles.

'That may do very weel for you,' said the old man, 'but whit will we dae for room if we get a popular preacher efter you?'

Fool's Way

Castle Huntly, Longforgan, at one time belonged to the Strathmore family of Glamis. The head of the house employed a fool as was the custom then. One day he asked the fool to take a message to Castle Huntly. The fool protested that it was a long way from Glamis to Longforgan and he had no horse to ride.

The Earl brought him a sapling and told him to 'ride on that.'

The fool arrived at his destination with the sapling between his legs as if it were a horse.

The sapling, an ash, was stuck in the ground opposite the gates where it is said to have grown and flourished for well over one hundred years.

THE SMUGGLERS

The Kirkinch Smugglers

There was a time in Scotland when people made their own whisky or bought it from a neighbour who had a still in a bothy near his home or even in the house itself.

From the early seventeenth century ever tighter laws were passed to put a stop to this, laws which were bitterly resented by the mass of folk who believed they had as much right to make their own whisky as they had to bake bannocks for the table.

Even more they resented the tax which successive governments placed on the whisky produced in the officially sanctioned distilleries which sprang up all over the Highlands and wherever the water was suitable.

To evade the tax, whisky-making went underground (often literally). All kinds of people, many of them otherwise law-abiding folk, set up their own secret stills or became customers of others who turned out the stuff on a large scale.

Whisky trails developed, routes by which the precious liquid was carried across country by horse or garron to supply the larger towns and villages where it was often too risky for the folk to make it themselves.

To put a stop to this, and to track down the illegal stills, the Government deployed a whole army of Excisemen, the gaugers, who rapidly became the most unpopular men in the country. It seems as if entire communities were determined to defy the law and avoid paying the duty on their glass of *uisquebeathe*.

The war between the gaugers and the people was particularly fierce in the early years of the nineteenth century. There are stories of that period from all over Scotland and several from the Sidlaws area are told by Stuart McHardy in his excellent book *Tales of Whisky and Smuggling*.

The passes through the Sidlaws were vital for the passage of spirits south to Dundee, Fife and beyond. The Excisemen knew this, and officers were permanently based in Blairgowrie, Alyth, Coupar Angus, Meigle and other towns and villages.

One of the places they kept an eye on was the little settlement of Kirkinch near the foot of Kinpurnie. The land here was very boggy, but the smugglers knew how to pick their way through the treacherous marshes and the route from Kirkinch to Hatton of Newtyle formed one stage of a secret and well-used whisky trail that led all the way from Strathspey to the south.

That is why a gauger called Gray was one evening lying hidden in the deep

*A gauger called Gray was one evening lying hidden in the deep bracken
on the slope of Kinpurnie…*

bracken on the slope of Kinpurnie. Wrapped in a blanket against the cold, he was watching, through a spyglass, all that was going on in the village.

He was particularly interested in the movements of a carter named Wright. On the surface Wright was an honest working man, but some of his journeys had Gray puzzled.

Wright had been away from home and Gray was watching for his return. And there he now was, coming up from the Dean Water on his cart with two men alongside him. In the gloaming Gray could just make out their faces and he gave an exclamation when he saw that one was a weel-kent smuggler from Donside, Charlie Grant by name.

The cart stopped at Wright's door and after looking around to see the coast was clear, the three lifted a tarpaulin revealing a large barrel which they proceeded to roll into the house.

As soon as they were inside, Gray rose from the bracken and hurried to Newtyle where his horse was tethered. He leaped into the saddle and rode hard to Coupar Angus to inform the Excise Superintendent, Henderson. If, as Gray suspected, Wright's house was a regular stopping-off place for smuggled whisky there might be several barrels under his roof.

Henderson decided it was too late to do anything that night. First thing in the morning he set off for Kirkinch accompanied by Gray and two other officers, Sutherland and Flowerden.

Soon they were hammering at Wright's door. When he opened it, Henderson and Gray shouldered their way in and began to search the rooms. Outside the other gaugers were looking in the cartshed and outhouses.

In the kitchen meal-kist Gray found a 'greybeard', a large jar full of spirits. It was a start.

'Right then,' smiled Henderson, 'you are under arrest. You may as well tell us where the rest is.'

Wright protested that he did not know what Henderson was talking about.

Just then Sutherland and Flowerden came in to say they had found nothing.

Henderson was furious. Were they too late? Had the whisky been moved on during the night?

Gray was looking around him. He felt certain it was hidden somewhere. His eye fell on what appeared to be a loose flagstone on the floor. He knelt down and drew out a knife. When he inserted it in the crevice the stone moved. He got his fingers under the stone and raised it up. Below, a ladder could be seen leading down to a dark cellar.

Flowerden took a lantern and held it over the hole. Peering down, the gaugers could make out around two dozen barrels ranged in rows.

Gray and Henderson were given no time to congratulate themselves. Three men had gathered in the doorway. One was Charlie Grant, the Donside smuggler. The others were also well known to the law: James McPherson and Peter McKay had had many brushes with the Excise. Now they faced the officers angrily.

To make matters worse there were shouts outside that told that a hostile crowd was gathering, local folk furious at this interference with their liquor supply.

Grant leered at the Superintendent. 'You will be leaving our *uisquebeathe* alone or it will be the worse for you,' he said.

Henderson drew himself up. 'You are meddling with an officer of the King in the performance of his duties. If you have any sense you will let us get on with it.'

Grant shouted with laughter, but Peter McKay stepped forward. 'Look,' he said, 'we're not wanting any trouble. I'm sure we can come to an agreement.'

Quietly and persuasively he pointed out to Henderson that he and his officers were outnumbered. They were not in a position to enforce the law. The smugglers had gone to a lot of trouble to bring the whisky this far and the crowd outside was not going to stand by and watch it taken away or destroyed.

His plan was this: Henderson need not go empty-handed. He could have the greybeard. While he carried that back to Coupar Angus the smugglers would move the barrels out of the district and nothing more need be said.

There was silence while Henderson considered the suggestion. He knew McKay was right: he and his men were hopelessly outnumbered. If he tried to arrest anyone the crowd outside would turn violent. But it went against the grain to let all those barrels go. The greybeard was not enough.

'I must have three of the barrels as well as the greybeard,' he said firmly.

Uproar broke out in the crowded room, and as word was passed around outside the crowd shouted in protest. Gray, Sutherland and Flowerden exchanged nervous glances.

Again it was McKay who quietened things down. He put forward another compromise. 'We'll give you one barrel and the greybeard,' he said.

Reluctantly, Henderson was forced to agree. He even consented, with bad grace, to lending one of the Excise horses which the smugglers promised they would return later to Coupar Angus.

Gray and his fellow gaugers could not get out of the hot, stuffy room quickly enough. Henderson was fuming, but the others were only too glad to have escaped from a tight corner.

However, the danger was not over yet. While the Excisemen were hurrying away, a furious quarrel sprung up behind them in Kirkinch. Grant and McPherson had not agreed with what had happened. They hated the gaugers so much they were opposed to them getting away with any whisky at all.

It was only too easy for them to rouse the passions of the younger and more hotheaded locals. McKay and Grant were powerless to stop them rushing off after the departing officers. They caught up with them just past Fullarton. The gaugers were walking alongside their horses when they heard running feet.

Out of the trees on either side of the track they came, seizing the reins of the horses carrying the whisky and pulling it away, while others beat the rest of the horses with sticks, sending them careering into the woods. The gaugers themselves were thrown to the ground and held till the whisky was well away. Their attackers then scattered with laughter and jeers.

Henderson was beside himself with rage. As soon as he reached Coupar Angus, footsore and breathless after hurrying all the way, he had warrants issued for the arrest of all the men he could name who had been involved in that day's work.

Then he called out the dragoons and, on a borrowed horse, rode back to Kirkinch. The house was empty and, needless to say, when they prised up the flagstone and descended into the cellar, there was not a trace of whisky to be found.

Some of the dragoons were left on guard and when Wright finally risked returning home he was seized and charged. He was to spend six months in prison.

In time Charlie Grant, McPherson and McKay were also tracked down and arrested. They each got nine months in gaol.

The sentences, you may think, were surprisingly light considering that the smugglers were caught red-handed at their illegal trade and remembering the rough treatment meted out to the Excise officers in Kirkinch and on the road to Coupar Angus. Whether they were enough to deter the convicted men from indulging in smuggling activities again, I cannot say.

Flushed Out

About a mile and a half west from the castle of Kinnaird is the waterfall known as Linn-ma-Gray (*Linne-mo-Ghraidh*, 'Linn of My Darling'). Charles Spence, the Carse poet, saw it as a romantic spot and he wrote a sentimental poem about it which is given at the end of this book (p.158).

In earlier times, however, this rocky gorge was a hideout for smugglers. They made illicit spirits there and hid it under the overhanging cliffs.

The Excisemen found out what was going on and ordered them to stop using it or suffer arrest. The smugglers went but left all their gear there, hoping to return.

It was wintertime and there came a heavy fall of snow followed by a sudden thaw. The upper stream was swollen and the waterfall was larger and faster than anyone remembered. The water surged down the gorge, flushing out all the equipment, smashing much of it and sending pots, pans and kegs tumbling down to the flat lands of the Carse.

But if the smugglers lost all their precious gear—and their store of whisky—there was some consolation for them. If they had been at Linn-ma-Gray at the time of the thaw they might have been swept to their deaths.

A Roadside Battle

In his *Annals of an Angus Parish* (1888), W. Mason Inglis tells stories of the whisky smugglers. He gives the exact date of one incident, 12 March 1813. On that day three Excise officers uncovered nine and a half ankers (95 gallons) of spirits in a field near Auchterhouse. Congratulating themselves they loaded it onto a cart and set off for Dundee.

They were well on their way when three Highlandmen burst from the side of the road and attacked them with sticks and stones. For an hour the customs men defended their precious cargo while the Highlanders made one attack after another.

When some farmers came along the officers thought they would receive some help. Not a bit of it: the farmers passed on and left them to it.

One of the Highlanders received a shot wound in the neck while a customs man had cuts to his head. The Excise party must have been relieved when the smugglers, having seized three and a half ankers, disappeared into the woods.

Mr Mason Inglis was minister of Auchterhouse at the end of the nineteenth century so he would have heard that and other stories at first hand from his parishioners.

In his *Annals* he tells how Government troops were once seen approaching one of the biggest Auchterhouse farms. The farmer was dismayed: he had a considerable quantity of illegal spirits stored on the premises.

By the time they knocked at his door he was well prepared. 'Come awa in, lads, come awa!' he greeted them.

He sat them down and regaled them with hefty drams which they knocked back gratefully, never dreaming it was contraband, exactly what they were looking for.

If they had glanced out of the window they would have seen the servants carrying away some very suspicious items. By the time the troopers had emptied their glasses and gone out to search the farm buildings there was nothing to be found.

Thirsty Work at Auchterhouse

In his book *Tales of Whisky and Smuggling*, Stuart McHardy relates several stories of the conflict that raged in the early nineteenth century between Excise officers trying to carry out their duties and people in and around the Sidlaws who were equally determined to thwart them.

Not only did local folk work hand in glove with smugglers using the 'whisky roads' through the hills, but many of them had their own stills despite the fact these were strictly illegal.

It seems they would do anything to protect them too. An Auchterhouse man, Davie Stewart, had built himself a still on a hill burn behind the village. He and his sons had several barrels of the spirits stacked inside and were filling yet another when the bothy door crashed open.

Standing there was an Exciseman called James McNicol, a Highlander who relished tracking down transgressors and bringing them to book. Behind him stood three officers.

McNicol pointed to the barrels. 'Hand over that whisky in the name of the King!' he ordered.

The response was not what he expected. Stewart and his sons, big men all of them, seized sticks and cudgels and rushed at the gaugers. Taken by surprise the officers fell back, but they were armed with staffs and once they had managed to draw them they struck hard and gradually got the upper hand, felling Stewart and one of his sons to the ground.

'Fetch the horses,' panted McNicol to his men. 'We'll take the barrels.'

At that moment, however, there was the sound of shouting. About a dozen local men had been working at another still higher up the burn. They had seen what was happening and were coming to the Stewarts' rescue.

They were still some way off but McNicol realised there was no hope of his being allowed to remove the whisky. Lifting a barrel he threw it on the rocks, breaking it open and yelling at his officers to do the same. Barrel after barrel was hoisted in the air and smashed on the rocks by the burn so that the water ran with spirits.

When all the barrels were smashed he fired a shot over the heads of the approaching mob, holding them at bay until his officers fetched the horses. Then they leaped on their backs and rose off quickly to safety.

Auchterhouse, McHardy tells us, was 'a hotbed of smuggling activity'. Not only did smuggler convoys pass through it coming from Glen Ogilvy on the other side of the range, but many of the locals, like the Stewarts, were engaged in the trade. He tells the story of a woman who, as a child, had been lying in bed when gaugers had come to the cottage door.

Her father was about to be caught red-handed with several containers of whisky and a bag of malt in the house. Before the men entered the room he whispered to the little girl, then lifted her and the mattress, pushed the incriminating evidence underneath and replaced the mattress and child on top of it.

When the gaugers came in they found the mother and father bending over the child anxiously. The wee girl moaned convincingly.

'What's wrong with her?' one of the officers asked.

'Oh, she has an awful fever. Here, feel her brow for yourself.'

He took the gauger's hand but the man pulled it away. Terrified of infection, he hurried from the room and signalled to the others to leave quickly.

'Many a good laugh we had at that afterwards,' said the woman who lived to a ripe age. Perhaps that early experience gave her a taste for adventure and law-breaking for she was engaged in the trade all her life. She enjoyed a drop of the stuff herself too!

A Winter's Tale

A convoy of ponies threaded its way through the moonlit Sidlaws. At its head was a Lochaber man, MacMaster, a giant figure who feared nothing and no one.

The ponies were laden with whisky and, as winter was settling in and Hogmanay not far off, there would be a ready market for the spirits in Dundee.

With the threat of snow on the wind, the smugglers were relieved to leave the hills behind them. In the bitter darkness they urged the ponies across Strathmartine, heading towards Bridgefoot where arrangements had been made to empty the barrels into smaller containers.

Suddenly a young voice called out. MacMaster peered into the blackness. A small boy appeared, breathless from running. He was the innkeeper's son from Downfield and his father had sent him with a message.

'The gaugers are waitin' for you. They're at Baldragon.'

James McNicol, scourge of the smugglers, had been given a tip-off that the convoy was on its way. With his men and a group of dragoons he was lying in ambush at Baldragon, ready to pounce. He should have known his large party would be spotted and word passed on.

MacMaster thanked the boy and sent him home. He knew what to do. He would make for Auchterhouse where he had friends who would help him.

One of them was Jeannie Gray. She had a still below her kitchen, a fine, large, roomy place. It would hold a good few barrels.

But he was out of luck.

'It's full up!' she wailed. It was already crammed with barrels of her own.

She had another idea. At the side of her house was a logpile, a huge stack of wood to see her through the winter.

In no time the smugglers were pulling the pile away. It didn't take them long to hide the barrels beneath it. Others were concealed in cellars, haystacks, even the dungheap.

As they hid the last barrel the snow came on, covering everything with its cloak of secrecy.

With a big hug for Jean, MacMaster hurried his men away. They returned to the Sidlaws where they found a couple of empty bothies, lit fires and settled down to wait.

McNicol meanwhile had realised his quarry had eluded him. He searched several places, including Auchterhouse, but his men found nothing. The truth was they were so cold they did not search as thoroughly as they should, while the dragoons were grumbling that all this was a waste of their time. He had to call off the search.

Up in the hills MacMaster knew the convoy could not risk taking the whisky further. He led his men homeward, but not before he had had a long talk with Jeannie Gray.

Over the next few weeks the whisky was carried into Dundee under the cartloads of peat and firewood the local men took regularly to the townsfolk. There was also a lot more milk than usual being delivered to the city by the womenfolk. If a gauger had taken a sniff at one of the milk pails he would have got a surprise...

This is another of the stories handed down from the days of smuggling and recorded by Stuart McHardy in *Tales of Whisky and Smuggling*.

Today Customs and Excise is still battling against the smuggling trade. Alcohol, cigarettes and drugs are all brought into this country and sold illegally. It is a huge multi-million pound business now, but where is the romance, the adventure?

On the Lighter Side

Drouthy Elders

On Sunday, 28 March, 1869, anyone standing on one of the Sidlaw summits would have seen a great plume of smoke rise from Strathmore. He might also have seen the flames that were engulfing Meigle Parish Kirk.

The damage was devastating. The folk of Meigle, however, wasted no time in making plans for rebuilding. Work was started very quickly, and just fifteen months after the fire, on 3 July 1870, the church was reopened.

To mark the occasion the delighted elders held a meeting in the village inn. Their excuse was that they wanted to discuss the new building. The truth was that they were in a mood to celebrate.

And celebrate they did. Several hours later they somehow came to the conclusion that the church, fine though it looked, was a little too far to the west.

Out they all trooped and, putting their shoulders to the wall, pushed as hard as they could. Looking upwards at the clouds scudding across the sky they thought it was the church and themselves that were on the move.

Satisfied they had shifted the building to where they wanted it they congratulated one another and returned to the inn for another round of drinks.

One man was very quiet, however. He sat looking thoughtful and no one noticed when he made his way unsteadily outside. He came back a few minutes later, a happy smile on his face and carrying his bonnet in his hand.

'I've just done a thing nane o' ye could do,' he declared. 'I lifted the kirk masel and pu'ed my bonnet frae oot alow it!'

Curiously a rather similar story is told of the church built to serve the parish of St Martin's in 1773. In its case the builder, John Donald, suspected, when the work was finished, that it was 'a wee thocht oot o' the straucht'.

He brooded on this at the celebration in the change-house to mark its completion. At last he led the local worthies out and supervised as they took up their positions to move it. After a lot of heaving and pushing he expressed himself satisfied that it was 'a'richt noo' and they all returned to the change-house.

The church stood for only sixty-nine years and it was said that this early move was the cause of its short life!

The Drunken Fiddle

John, the fiddler, was a popular figure in Strathmore, in great demand at barn dances, weddings and other social occasions.

He liked a dram and played all the better for it. One night he was a bit more unsteady than usual, and as he made his way home his precious fiddle slipped from under his arm and plunged into a pool. As he retrieved it he was heard to exclaim, 'Ech, ech, fiddle, ye hae seen *me* often fu', but I never saw *you* fu' afore!'

This Little Pig...

An old woman in Kirkinch had a young pig which took ill and lay down as if dead. It was buried just outside the Kirkyaird wall but the very next morning its owner got the shock of her life when she opened the door and the pig ran inside, having dug its way out of its 'grave'.

The woman was too afraid to keep it but a neighbour had no such qualms. She looked after it for many years and it had numerous progeny. Its original owner, however, never looked its way again.

Devil's Work

A minister in the village of Ardler one day passed a woman carrying a young sow. It was struggling in her arms and he heard her say, 'The Devil choke ye, beast!'

At the other end of the village he came on another woman trying to drive a flock of ducklings through a stable door.

'Devil tak ye, will ye no gang in?' she exclaimed.

He stopped and said to her, 'Ye'll hae tae wait a wee. The De'il's busy wi' a sow!'

Strange Echoes

The Priest of Kinfauns

Somewhere around Kinfauns, waiting to be rediscovered, there may lie a golden prize.

It belonged, they say, to a one-time priest or minister in the village, and there are different versions of what exactly happened. One is that he had left his home one morning to walk to the church, when, looking back, he saw his house disappear into the ground. The hole that was left filled up with water, forming a loch.

Another tradition claims that he was in the house when it sank and he went down with it.

According to a poem by David Millar, writing in Perth in the nineteenth century, this extraordinary occurrence was a punishment to the priest whom he links with a nun from the convent at Elcho. Millar's scurrilous verses treat the matter in a jocular manner but in earlier years it was taken very seriously indeed.

A rumour had got about amongst local people that the house had contained a golden cradle. The villagers took to going to the little loch—Loch Kaitre they called it—and staring into its waters hoping for a glimpse of gold.

At last they determined to drain the loch in the hope of uncovering the lost house and the wonderful cradle. They were well on their way with the task when somebody gave a shout. Glancing behind them they saw that their houses were on fire.

They stopped work and ran to save their homes, only to find it had been an illusion: there was not a flame to be seen. By the time they returned to Loch Kaitre it had again filled up with water.

After that they thought it better to leave the cradle where it was. In later years the landowner did what they had attempted to do. He drained off the water, apparently finding nothing of interest.

But could the sunken house and its golden cradle still be lying there hidden under the ground?

It is interesting to note that another golden cradle is said to lie at the bottom of a pool at Abernethy, in Fife. It belonged to the Pictish royal family and was flung there by a nursemaid to prevent the Scots from capturing it.

The Pitlyal Echo

One day, some years ago, a young man sat down on a little hill above the loch of Pitlyal in the Sidlaws. He had his shepherd's pipe with him and he decided that this was a good place to practise on it, away from all ears.

He raised the pipe to his lips and began to play, but when he paused a strange thing happened. He heard the notes repeated again—and again—and again. Three times he heard them and that was enough for him. He started to his feet and looked all around him. There was no one to be seen. It must be the Devil himself.

He stared at the pipe in his hand and then, terrified, snapped it in two. He ran from the spot and never played music again.

What he did not know was that any sound made on that hill—a shout, a cough, a sneeze—was liable to be heard repeated three times, thanks to the Pitlyal Echo. His friends told him about this but he would have none of it. As far as he was concerned the Devil himself had been in the Sidlaws that day.

The Stolen Bell

It is a long time since a bell rang out from the church of the Blessed Virgin near Westown, south of Kinnaird. If the story told of it is true, the bell that once hung here had the sweetest sound imaginable. It would carry, no doubt, well up the slopes of the Sidlaws as well as over the Carse with its scattered farms.

On one of these farms it was listened to, day after day, by someone who longed, increasingly, to possess it for himself. Not only did he love the sound of it, but perhaps he thought, too, that it would bring him a blessing.

At last, one night, he crept out and made his way stealthily to the church. Quickly he climbed up the belfry, lifted down the bell and carried it off home. He hid it in his house and went to bed.

Next morning he was amazed to wake up and hear the bell ringing out from the church as usual. He hurried to where he had hidden it the night before; it was gone.

Unable to believe what had happened, the farmer waited till nightfall and crept back to the church. Again he climbed the belfry, took down the bell and brought it home.

In the morning, once again, he was wakened by the bell ringing out as usual.

That night he returned to the church and once more stole the bell. Surely this time the bell would be his. He concealed it in the farmhouse with extra care.

In the morning he awoke and listened. No bell. He laughed with delight. He rose and went to look at it and gloat over this wonderful thing that was now his.

It had gone! He searched the whole house but it was nowhere to be seen. He rushed down to the church and looked up at the belfry—it was not there either. Soon people were gathering in groups and talking about the disappearance of their beloved bell. Everyone in the parish joined in the hunt for it but the bell was never found.

Here is the strangest thing of all though. Just over the fields from the church stands Inchmartine House. Every time a Laird of Inchmartine was about to die or be struck by disaster, people used to hear the pure note of their bell pealing as though from the sky.

But the belfry of the church of the Blessed Virgin remained empty and now the once lovely little building is a ruin.

The Dragon's Hole

Kinnoull Hill, viewed from the south, is, in my opinion, one of the great sights of Perthshire. Its wooded slopes rise steeply to high, rugged cliffs as impressive as any in the county. I just wish that the thousands who speed past the hill on that side, on the Dundee and southbound roads, had more chance to enjoy its beauty.

It is well worth finding a stopping place, perhaps at Walnut Grove, and taking time to admire it. In high summer the deep, rich woods are a joy, but at all times of year there are fresh pleasures and it is when the trees are bare of their leaves that you may catch a glimpse of one of Kinnoull's most intriguing features, a black hole up on the face.

The Dragon's Hole or Den is a cave once regarded with awe by the people of Perth. Earliest man may well have known and used the cave; there is no saying what took place here in the dawn of history. Later it was given Christian significance. St Serf, it was said, had killed a fearsome dragon that lived in the cave.

Serf is associated with several places, Culross, Airthrey and Dysart among them. The village of Dunning claimed that it was there he killed the dragon, but Perth folk disagreed. Wherever it took place, the event was recorded by the early chronicler Thomas Wyntoun, who said that the beast was slain by the power of prayer and that where it was killed 'that plas was ay the dragowny's den cald to this day'.

There is no cave at Dunning, though it has a neighbourhood still known as The Dragon. The cave on Kinnoull, on the other hand, looks every inch a dragon's lair. Looking up at it one can easily imagine a foul creature slithering from that dark mouth and descending the precipitous slopes to terrorise the locals. (A dragon in Scottish folklore is a snake or giant worm, not the fire-breathing kind.)

In pre-Reformation times the cave was a place of pilgrimage in spring when a Festival of the Dragon was held there on a Sunday in May. People must have been fleeter of foot then, or the approach to it has worsened with the passing years.

This religious celebration was, like so many others, banned by the dark-browed Reformers. It was not so easy to stop it, however, and some years later the Kirk Session had this Act read from the pulpits and proclaimed at the Cross:

> Because the assembly of ministers and elders understand that the resort to the Dragon Hole, both by young men and women with their piping, and drums sticking before them, through the town, has raised no small slander to this congregation, not without suspicion of filthiness following thereupon: the said assembly, for avoiding thereof in times to come, have, with consent of the magistrates of this town, statute and ordained that no person, whether man or woman, of this congregation shall resort or repair hereafter to the Dragon Hole, as they have done in times past—namely in the month of May—nor shall pass through the town, in this way to it, with piping and

striking of drums, as heretofore they have done, under the pain of twenty shillings to the poor, to be paid by every person, as well men or women, that shall be found guilty; also that they shall make their public repentance upon a Sabbath day, in the presence of the people.

One gets the impression that it was the music-making and the thought that the folk were actually enjoying themselves at the Festival which so rankled with the killjoys of the Kirk. They found the Festival hard to stamp out for they were still punishing people for taking part several years later.

The Dragon's Hole is referred to in a poem by Henry Adamson, one of Perth's earliest writers, in 1638. This refers to a tradition that a magic stone, bestowing the gift of invisibility, was once found in the cave. Later, the finder lost it and it was never recovered.

The poem bears the odd title 'The Muses' Threnody, or Mirthful Mournings on the Death of Mr Gall'. Gall, a Perth merchant, had died at an early age of consumption. Adamson himself was to die the following year.

The eminent poet, William Drummond of Hawthornden, had been impressed by 'The Muses' Threnody', admiring it particularly for its references to the antiquities of Perth. In a letter to Adamson he wrote, 'Happy hath Perth been in such a citizen, not so other towns of this kingdom, by want of so diligent a searcher and preserver of their fame from oblivion.'

In the poem Adamson has these lines:

> Meanwhile our boat, by Freertown hole doth slide,
> Our course not stopped with the flowing tide,
> We need not card, nor crostaffe for our pole,
> But from thence landing clam' the Dragon Hole,
> With crampets on our feet and clubs in hand,
> Where it's recorded James Keddie fand
> A stone enchanted like to Gyges' ring,
> Which made him disappear, a wondrous thing
> If it had been his hap to have retained it,
> But losing it, again could never find it.

Gyges was a shepherd in Lydia who, according to Plato, went into a deep chasm and found a brazen horse. It contained the body of a man with a ring on his finger. Gyges took the ring and discovered that, when he wore it, he was invisible.

Gyges achieved wealth through his find, murdering the King of Lydia and marrying his widow. James Keddie was not so clever. However, in spite of what Adamson says, it appears Keddie never actually found an enchanted stone.

One version of the story has it that the stone was supposed to have been lost on Kinnoull by a stranger riding on the hill. The rumour spread and Keddie, a tailor, was one of many who scoured the hill in search of it.

Even 'the Lady of Kinnoull' caught the fever and went wandering on the slopes with her attendants, all pouncing on every stone that gleamed and saying to one another, 'I see ye. See ye me?'

Most people quickly tired of the search, but not Keddie: he was determined to find it. Some Perth worthies decided to play a trick on him. One of them followed him and put the usual question: 'I see ye. See ye me?'

'I see ye,' said Keddie.

The man still followed him and when Keddie bent and picked up a pebble with a bit of a shine to it, he pretended that Keddie had vanished. 'Where are ye, sir?' he asked in feigned surprise. 'I canna see ye!'

Keddie was overjoyed. He went home in jubilation, convinced he had found the magic stone.

He then did something very foolish: he decided to walk through the streets of Perth stark-naked. The street urchins gathered round him jeering and hitting him with sticks and when he turned and fled, outraged citizens threw stones after him.

His dream of invisibility was over.

I was surprised, when I started to make enquiries about the Dragon's Hole, how few people in Perth had ever heard of it. I found only one person who had actually visited it and that was some time ago. No doubt its awkward site has a lot to do with this. The climb is steep and the ascent at any point on this face of Kinnoull can be extremely dangerous.

There is a tradition that William Wallace and some of his men once hid in the cave. True or not, the Dragon's Hole is today left with its memories and secrets.

On the Lighter Side

Wrong Answer

In the 1830s the minister in Meigle was the Rev. James Mitchell while the minister of Bendochy was a Mr Honey.

In company Mr Mitchell once put this question to a group of ladies: 'Why is Meigle Presbytery like a bees' skeep?'

The answer he wanted was that there was Honey in it. Instead one lady floored him with the reply, 'Because it has so many drones!'

In a Hole

It was a beadle of Meigle church who had this unfortunate experience. He had been asked to dig an extra deep grave and was down at the bottom of it when some joker pulled up his ladder.

Furious, he shouted and swore at the top of his voice. As fate would have it the first person to hear him was the minister.

'Oh, man,' he said, 'No good can come of swearing. Will ye repent?'

'Repent!' shouted the beadle. 'Repent! Ye telt us only last Sunday that there was no repentance in the grave!'

No Sin

The strangest arguments start up in pubs. Once, in Meigle, a farmer insisted that it would be no sin to burn Bibles. A kirk elder who was in the company was equally insistent that it would be a terrible sin.

The argument raged on with the farmer maintaining that burning Bibles was no worse than pulling down an old church no longer in use.

'No, no,' said the elder, 'for the kirk is naething but stane and lime.'

'Aye,' said the farmer, 'and the Bible is juist paper and ink!'

Tales from History

The Flight of the Hawk

The Battle of Luncarty has never caught the public imagination. I doubt if many people make their way to the village north of Perth specially to seek out the battle site. Probably it is just too distant a conflict, too remote a cause.

Yet it mattered greatly at the time. The Danes, in the tenth century, were a constant threat with their raids into Scotland. They had been driven out before, but this time they had mounted an even more determined invasion. Having landed at Montrose they rampaged through Angus, leaving a trail of destruction.

The King of the time, Kenneth II, was at Stirling when the news was brought to him. He at once made preparations to meet the invaders head on. He summoned his army and led them north. The Danes had got as far as Luncarty, and that was where the two forces met, on the banks of the Tay.

Battle commenced and both sides fought hard without either making any headway. Then there was a shift: the Danes began to gain the upper hand. They broke through the Scots defences and were close to surrounding Kenneth and his group of nobles. The situation was critical; if the King and his leaders were to die, Scotland would be at the mercy of the Danes.

It was at this point that there occurred, if tradition is to be believed, a startling intervention. A peasant called Hay had been watching the conflict from the other side of the Tay where he had been working in the field with his two sons.

Seeing the danger to the King, Hay seized the coulter (or cutter) of his plough, called to his sons and led them across the river. As they clambered out of the water on to the bank they saw that the Scots were falling back, leaving the King exposed. Hay shouted to the soldiers not to retreat but to turn and fight. He started laying into the enemy right and left with the coulter, backed up by his sons who had armed themselves with rough weapons before following their father.

Soon Hay and his boys were in the forefront of the Scots, leading them forward. The Danes were driven further and further back until, the spirit gone out of them, they turned and scattered.

As the Scots celebrated their victory on the field, Kenneth called for Hay and thanked him warmly. He did more than that. He rewarded him with the offer of lands in the Carse of Gowrie. The lands would start at Kinnoull but where they finished would depend on a hawk. The bird was to be released from Kinnoull and its flight followed. Where it came down would be the boundary of Hay's estate.

In due course Hay released the hawk at Kinnoull and watched it circle in the air

78

and then head off along the Carse. It did not alight until it came to St Madoes and there it dropped down and perched on a stone.

This, according to the tale, was how the Hays acquired their estate in the Carse where they were to live and prosper as Earls of Errol for generations. It was the 10th Earl who brought it all to an end when he sold the lands to pay off heavy debts.

The Hawk Stane, on which the bird perched when it came down, can still be seen at St Madoes. The flight of the hawk is remembered while the Battle of Luncarty is all but forgotten.

A Timely Rescue

William the Lion. The name makes him sound very courageous indeed. In fact he was more rash than brave and his foolhardiness got him into a lot of trouble. He was probably called 'the Lion' because he seems to have been the first to use the now familiar Scottish lion rampant on his banner.

His sister married Gilchrist, 3rd Earl of Mar, but in a fit of jealousy her husband murdered her. William punished him heavily. He stripped Mar and all his family of their wealth and poured much of it into the building of Arbroath Abbey.

Tradition tells how, year later, William was on a hunting expedition in Glen Ogilvy, unaware that Mar's three sons were in hiding there. The youths were watching William from a distance, but keeping out of sight, and they saw him fall behind the rest of the party.

He was riding along on his own when a group of bandits suddenly appeared and attacked him. He would have been overpowered and killed if the Gilchrists had not rushed in and scattered them.

The king thanked his rescuers profusely and asked them who they were. He was astonished to learn that they were his own nephews whom he had outlawed along with their father.

In gratitude he gave them back much of the property he had confiscated. Glen Ogilvy itself he gifted to their uncle, Gilbert, and the family dropped the hated name of Gilchrist and called themselves Ogilvy (or Ogilvie) instead. It is said that most Angus folk of that name are descended from these young men.

Glen Ogilvy today is still something of the secret place it was when the three brothers chose to hide there. I could see no signpost to it when I went to look for it and its scattered farms have a lost and lonely air. It is just a pity that its charm is somewhat marred by the modern ironmongery on the summit of Craigowl.

Wallace's Escape

William Wallace was living at Kilspindie when he was involved in an incident in Dundee that can be said to have set his feet on the course they were to follow and so change the shape of Scotland's history.

Wallace had been brought up in Renfrewshire but had been sent to the Sidlaw village in his early teens to stay with his uncle, a priest. The reason usually given for his being there is that he was to complete his education in Dundee. There may have been another reason: Edward I was tightening his hold on Scotland and it is highly possible that his father, Sir Malcolm Wallace, thought his son would be safer there. Scotland had become a dangerous place for those who resented the English occupation. The fact that Wallace's mother joined him at Kilspindie strengthens this theory. She, too, would be safer in this rural retreat.

If Sir Malcolm feared his headstrong son might one day land himself in trouble, he was right. For an account of what happened I have gone back to the proceedings of the Society of Antiquaries of Scotland for 1900. In this appeared a paper by a local researcher, Alexander Hutcheson, FSA (Scot). He had been shown a manuscript kept at Castle Huntly and lent him by the then proprietor, a man called Paterson. The manuscript, written about 1760, was signed 'A Gardener', and Hutcheson admits he had no idea if this was the writer's surname, a pseudonym, or his occupation at the castle!

It was, however, the earliest local reference to the Wallace incident that Hutcheson had found and I am inclined to believe it may be a lot more credible than the numerous versions written since.

All accounts agree that Wallace lost his temper with a young man named Selbie and killed him. Selbie is usually described as the son of the Governor of the English garrison at Dundee Castle. This manuscript describes him as the son of 'the Mayor of Dundee' which is probably much the same thing. According to it, young Selbie was a fellow pupil at the Dundee School. His father was 'a Yorkshire Gentleman'.

This is how it says the incident arose:

> On day when all the Schoolars was at play at the West Port of that town Young Selbie found fault with Wallace for having a suit of short Green Clothes with a belt from thence depended a Durk or Skene. This weapon is still practised in Scotland and is very Dangerous in Close Combat, it serves for manual uses as well as for Defence; it is ten Inches Long in the Blade and two edged with a row of holls up the middle, the handle is five Inches Long, it hings befor on the Belly—this Weapon young Selbie wanted from Wallace at any rate, so that a scuffle inshued between the two young Heroes.

It developed into more than a 'scuffle'. Wallace wrestled his opponent to the ground but Selbie kept coming back at him, furious that Wallace would not meekly submit and hand him the weapon he wanted. Four times Wallace had him on his back. When Selbie rose and attacked him a fifth time Wallace drew the 'Skene' which was the cause of the fight. He stabbed the youth to the heart.

At once realising the seriousness of what he had done, Wallace fled from the scene. He ran to a house 'on the Northside of the Overgate', presumably the home of friends. A woman is credited with sheltering him there while troops from the garrison scoured the streets and 'vended their fury on the inhabitants of the town'. According to 'A Gardener' they would have laid Dundee in ashes had not Sir John Scrimger of Dudhope appealed to them to stop.

She quickly took off her loose spinning jacket and told him to slip it on…

Wallace could not stay indefinitely in hiding in Dundee. Apart from anything else his mother and uncle must have been desperate for news of him. He was smuggled out by the West Port and started to walk as swiftly as he could towards Kilspindie.

The Gardener manuscript says little about what happened next, but the story has been well recorded and I have gone to other sources for the details.

Hurrying away from the town Wallace was exhausted as he passed through Longforgan. Seeing a stone outside a cottage he sat down to rest on it.

The cottage belonged to a couple called Smith who had a small croft. Mr Smith worked the croft while his wife spun cloth. That day, as she was seated at the spinning, she heard footsteps pass the door and stop. She rose and looked out of the door and saw a tired youth resting on the stone.

She questioned him and he told her what had happened and that soldiers from the castle would certainly be after him. They would have found out where he lived and would be following him along the Carse.

'Come in,' she said. Inside she quickly took off her loose spinning jacket and told him to slip it on and put a shawl over his head. Then she sat him at the spinning.

He had not long started when the door was thrown open and troops came in. They were calling at every cottage on the road. They searched the rooms and questioned Mrs Smith but took little notice of the figure bent over 'her' work.

After they had gone, Mr Smith came in from the fields to see what was happening. The couple gave Wallace bread and milk and a bed to sleep on. He rested there until after dark when he resumed his journey.

It must have been a huge relief to his mother and uncle when he reached Kilspindie, but of course he could no longer stay there. It is said that his uncle helped the two escape by dressing them in the guise of pilgrims going to the shrine of St Margaret at Dunfermline. They crossed the Tay to Lindores and made their way southwards to safety.

Dundee has long been rightly proud of its connection with Wallace. On the wall outside the Episcopal Cathedral Church of St Paul, in the heart of the city, is a plaque bearing, amongst other historical information, these words:

Site of the Castle of Dundee destroyed cir. 1314. Near this spot William Wallace struck the first blow for Scottish Independence cir. 1288.

In all the accounts I have read of the affair I have never seen a word of sympathy for the foolish but sadly unfortunate young Selbie!

The vicinity of the plaque would have been an ideal spot for a statue of Wallace— the only one perhaps showing him as a youth rather than a bearded warrior. Instead, close by is the stocky figure of a later fighting hero, Admiral Duncan, who won a famous victory over the Dutch at Camperdown off the Netherlands coast in 1797.

So what else can be seen to remind us of this stirring episode in the life of Wallace? What about the stone on which he sat to rest outside the Smiths' cottage? It is salutary to reflect that had he not paused there and been taken in by the Smiths he would very likely have been captured and put to death.

I knew from old books that there were in fact two stones. The main one was hollow and was a quern or bear stone, used for unhusking the bear, a primitive type of barley. This stood outside the Smiths' door and was covered by a flat stone to keep it clean inside and for use as a seat.

For a description of how the receptacle was used I go back to Mr Hutcheson's paper and a quote he obtained from a minister of Grandtully, Perthshire, the Rev. John Maclean:

'The dry barley grains were put into the stone pot or knocking-stone, sprinkled with a little water to moisten them and to soften the husk, and then beaten with a wooden mallet or mell until the husks were rubbed off. If the day was dry and a wind blowing, the contents of the stone pot would be taken out and laid on a cloth or any little knoll or dry place to get the husks blown away, or sometimes, and especially if it was wet weather or no wind blowing, the barley was put into a 'wecht' (a sheepskin stretched over a hoop) and shaken up and down, the husks meanwhile being vigorously blown away by the breath. This would be repeated until all the husks were blown away. By this primitive method the barley intended for broth was prepared down to as recently as 1850 in some districts in the Highlands.

'The wooden mallet was sometimes shaped like a pestle, and in use was simply lifted up and down with pounding motion; more frequently the mallet was fixed in a wood handle axe-wise, and was then used like a hammer. Sometimes the mallet was double-headed, having a broad or ball-head at each end of a stem, like a dumb-bell, and having the handle fixed at a right angle to the middle of the stem.

'The advantage of this arrangement was thought to be that as the ball-ends, from being used at intervals alternately, got to be worn to a slightly different superficies, they imparted, when alternated, a sort of rotatory motion to the grains of barley which contributed to unhusking, besides making a better balanced hammer than the one-sided form.'

I have used the quotation at length to illustrate that the quern is interesting in itself as an artefact of rural life.

The quern and its covering stone continued to sit outside the Longforgan cottage long after the Smiths had passed on. Their descendants still lived there and passed on the croft from one generation to the next.

According to the Rev. Adam Philip, once the minister at Longforgan and the author of *Songs and Sayings of Gowrie*, the stones did not leave their position at the cottage door until 1862 when a descendant handed them into the care of the Laird of Castle Huntly.

From other sources I know that not everyone locally was happy when the historic stones, for so long a village landmark, disappeared into the castle. It was felt that they should be accessible to the public.

I tracked them down to the McManus Museum and Galleries in Dundee where they are kept in safe custody although, alas, at the time of writing this, they are not on view. Mr Adrian Zealand of the Museum kindly gave me information about the stones but was not able to let me see them as they were in store, in a crate, in the bowels of the building. I would like to think that by the time this book is published the stones will be on permanent display either at the MacManus or elsewhere in the area.

At least they are safe. In *Historic Scenes in Perthshire* William Marshall laments the loss of what was known as Wallace's Cave in the Den of Pitroddie. He says the cave used to draw many visitors. It was big enough to hold about a dozen people and was firmly believed locally to have provided Wallace with a hiding-place on one of his exploits. It is, of course, highly likely he would have known the whereabouts of the cave from the time he spent at Kilspindie as a schoolboy.

What happened to the cave? Marshall says that a quarry was opened close by. It supplied Dundee with whinstone blocks but, unfortunately, as the work proceeded, detritus began to pile up in front of the cave entrance.

Appeals were made for a protective wall to be built in front of the cave—some of the whinstone blocks could have been spared—but nothing was done and it was gradually submerged until completely buried.

Marshall hoped that some future excavator might 'disinter it'. It has not happened yet, but why not?

The Laird and the Preacher

When Charles II regained the throne in 1660 he restored episcopacy to the Scottish church despite having signed the National Covenant some years earlier.

Rather than comply, many ministers led their flocks out of the churches and took to holding services wherever they could: in halls, barns, or even in the open air, the famous conventicles.

These could vary from tiny groups to huge gatherings. News of the time and place would be spread by word of mouth only. Secrecy was vital lest troops be sent in to break it up and arrest the ringleaders.

The preachers themselves were in the greatest danger. The more popular and successful they were, the bigger the risk they ran. Capture could mean imprisonment and possibly death.

Many of the lairds favoured episcopacy and looked on the preachers as rebels and troublemakers. Some of them would turn a blind eye to conventicles in the vicinity of their homes, but others would report them to the authorities or even ride in with a few trusted men and break up the gatherings.

Such a man was the Laird of Megginch. One time word had reached him that a particularly popular preacher was to hold a conventicle not far from the castle on a certain date. He was determined to break it up and, if possible, arrest the preacher.

The night before the conventicle he overheard laughter coming from the servants' hall. A strange voice intrigued him, and he asked one of his servants who was there. He was told it was a stranger, a wandering man who had come to the door seeking shelter for the night. This was no unusual thing in those days and the servants had brought him in and set a meal in front of him. To their delight he was proving great company.

The servant hurried back to join the others and later the Laird, curious to meet this fellow who was proving so popular, strolled through to the hall.

True enough, the man had a pleasant, cheerful personality and a ready wit. The Laird warmed to him. He told him he was looking forward to the next day as he knew there was to be a conventicle and he intended to have good sport interrupting it and arresting the preacher.

'If that is your purpose,' said the stranger, 'I can be of service to you. I know the man who is to preach. Let me come with you to the service. As soon as it's over I will bring the man to you and you can deal with him as you think proper.'

The Laird thanked him and went to bed well satisfied. With his guest's help he looked forward to apprehending the villainous preacher.

Next day, when he was ready to ride to the conventicle, the stranger joined him. They set off into the Sidlaws and before long were looking down into a sheltered hollow where a crowd had gathered. As he rode down into the throng he was annoyed to recognise many of his own tenants. They fell back and looked at him fearfully, but he meant them no harm. It was the preacher he was after.

Where was he? He looked about him eagerly. Suddenly he was aware that his companion was advancing to the front. What was he doing? He saw him reach into his pocket and pull out a Bible. Then he began to address the gathering.

At first the Laird was furious. To think he had given this rogue shelter under his roof! But as his anger cooled he began to listen to what the man was saying. He even found himself joining in the prayers and the singing.

When the service concluded the preacher walked straight through the crowd and stood before the Laird.

'I have come to fulfill my part of the bargain,' he said simply. 'I put myself in your hands.'

The Laird smiled. 'I have changed my mind,' he said. 'From this day I will put no hindrance on the holding of conventicles. As for you, you are a free man. Go in peace.'

The preacher's name was William Reid and he was later to become the minister of Dunning where he was well loved for many years.

The Hill of the Ants

Considering its world-wide fame, Dunsinnan Hill is really not much to look at. Notice I am using the local spelling which accords with local pronunciation. Elsewhere they can spell it 'Dunsinane' if they want. 'Dunsinane', with the stress on the first and third syllables, is a clumsy cratur compared with the Perthshire native's 'Dunsinnan' in which the accent is on the middle syllable. Just say them one after the other and savour the difference. 'Dunsinane' is full of stops and starts while 'Dunsinnan' flows off the tongue. It has poetry and music in it.

Still, I have to admit it's pretty disappointing as a hill. It doesn't stand out in the range the way some of the others do—Kinpurnie, for instance, or Craigowl, or King's Seat, or Auchterhouse. It sits on too tight a site, close to two roads and squeezed between the aptly-named Black Hill and—to the horror, I imagine, of many visitors—a large quarry. Why this was ever permitted so close to the famous summit I cannot think. Only strenuous opposition a few years ago prevented it biting even closer.

Despite its international fame there is no attempt to 'sell' Dunsinnan. Visitors must find their way to it virtually unaided. If they are lucky they will find a corner to park in and then it's a short easy climb. The best approach is from just outside the village of Collace.

What do they find at the top? Traces of a building, the outlines of ramparts. Not much, but enough to stir the imagination since these are generally believed to be the remains of Macbeth's Castle, the place where he received warning of the enemy's advance from Birnam Hill twelve miles away under the camouflage cover of green branches.

Shakespeare, of course, muddied the waters, and we can take precious little from his play as fact. However, it seems Macbeth did occupy a hill fort here, and on a day in July, 1054, led his men down to engage Malcolm, son of Duncan, in battle.

Local tradition likes to have it that Macbeth died in the fighting or soon after; he didn't. He lived for another three years until Malcolm finally caught up with him at Lumphanan, Aberdeenshire.

In Sir Walter Scott's *Tales of a Grandfather* the story of Macbeth runs on similar lines to Shakespeare's, three witches (from Forres) and all. Duncan's murder by the Macbeths takes place in 'a great castle near Inverness'. He has Macbeth, now the King, harbouring a secret hatred and fear of Macduff, the Thane of Fife, who, he thinks, will join forces with Malcolm if the latter ever returns to Scotland from English exile.

Macduff is wary of Macbeth and feels safe only when he is behind the stout walls of his home, Kennoway Castle, Fife. When he receives an invitation to visit Macbeth's new castle of Dunsinnan he is alarmed but dares not refuse. A request by Macbeth was regarded as a command; he and other nobles had already been 'asked' to provide oxen to help bring the building materials to Dunsinnan and all had obeyed. Now, ostensibly, Macbeth wants to show off his new castle. Some form of entertainment to celebrate the near-completion of the fort is planned.

When Macduff and the other guests arrive they find that building work is still going on; the castle is being made even bigger and stronger.

Macbeth himself is supervising operations. Next day he rides out with some of his attendants to watch the various pairs of oxen dragging wood and stones up the slope of Dunsinnan. It is a hot day and some of the beasts are struggling with their heavy loads. One pair catches his eye: they are very slow and so tired they fall to the ground.

Macbeth demands to know who, among his guests, sent beasts so weak that they could not carry out the work.

'Macduff, the Thane of Fife,' is the reply.

'Then,' says an angry Macbeth, 'since the Thane of Fife sends such worthless cattle as these to do my labour, I will put his own neck into the yoke, and make him drag the burdens himself.'

A friend of Macduff's overhears these words and hurries up to the castle. He finds Macduff in the hall and reports what has happened. Macduff has been about to sit down to dinner but he does not wait. He snatches a loaf of bread from the table, calls for his servants and horses and gallops off in the direction of Fife.

When he reaches a river ferry crossing he finds to his dismay that he has left in so great a hurry that he does not have enough to pay for it. He gives the ferryman the loaf of bread instead, and the crossing thereafter is known as the Ferry of the Loaf.

An early reference suggests the crossing as being over the River Earn, but it is much more likely to have been the Tay, and a claim is made for what was known as the Heughhead ferry from the old Cairnie pier, near Pitfour Castle, to Ferryfield, Carpow.

Macbeth, having learned of Macduff's flight, sets off in hot pursuit determined to hunt him down and kill him. He follows him across Fife but when he reaches Kennoway it is Lady Macduff who looks down from the castle walls.

Macbeth shouts to her to open the gates. Macduff must give himself up forthwith or they both will suffer the consequences.

Lady Macduff is unperturbed by his threats. 'Do you see,' she says, 'yon white sail upon the sea? Yonder goes Macduff to the Court of England. You will never see him again till he comes back with young Prince Malcolm to pull you down from the throne and put you to death. You will never put your yoke, as you threatened, on the Thane of Fife's neck.'

Scott finishes this story: 'Some say that Macbeth was so much incensed at this bold answer that he and his guards attacked the castle and took it, killing the brave lady and all whom they found there. Others say, I believe more truly, that the King, seeing that the fortress of Kennoway was very strong and that Macduff had escaped from him and was embarked for England, departed back to Dunsinane without attempting to take the castle. The ruins are still to be seen and are called the "Thane's Castle".'

Macbeth is remembered in a number of traditions which lingered on for long afterwards in the countryside around Dunsinnan. One is that Macduff's army attacked the fort and that Macbeth fled on to King's Seat, found he could not escape and leaped from it to die on the rocks below. He was then buried under a large stone in what is known as the Lang Man's Grave.

Another version is that it is not Macbeth who lies buried there but one of his leaders. A third story was that a market used to be held around the site and that a very tall man always pitched his tent on the same spot. He was known as the Lang Man and over the years he amassed a lot of money from his dealings.

One night he disappeared and his money with him. It was believed he had been robbed and murdered and his body hidden under the long stone where his tent had always stood.

The people of Meigle lay claim to Macbeth's grave. The tradition here is that he and his followers retreated under Macduff's onslaught, fled northward along the back of the Sidlaws, then turned to face the enemy between Meigle and Newtyle. A mound named Belliduff is said to be his tomb. To confuse matters, one of his high-ranking officers is said to lie under what is called Macbeth's Stone.

There are other Macbeth connections in the district. Just north of Dunsinnan rises Macbeth's Law while at Cairnbeddie, between Guildtown and St Martin's, they claim to have the site of Macbeth's first castle where he lived for ten years.

At Cairnbeddie he had two celebrated witches as neighbours, one at Collace and the other near Dunsinnan, and it's said he sought their advice when considering where to build his new castle. It was they who advised him to site it on Dunsinnan.

The stone used was not local but said to have been brought from Angus and elsewhere.

The experts may disagree, but one derivation offered for the name Dunsinnan is 'The Hill of the Ants', the reason being that so many men and oxen were employed on the building of the castle, the hill looked, from a distance, like a busy antheap.

Another quite different tradition associates Dunsinnan with the Stone of Destiny. One of the many legends surrounding the Stone is that it was buried on the slopes of the hill to save it from falling into the clutches of Edward I, and that the stone he carried back in triumph to England was a false substitute.

It is claimed by some that the Stone was unearthed last century, and while some reports say it was reburied on the same spot, others maintain it was taken away and 'lost'. I like to think it still lies there and that the drab chunk of sandstone now resting in state in Edinburgh Castle is an imposter.

A ravine lies between Dunsinnan and the Black Hill. Overlooking the ravine on the Black Hill is a jutting-out rock called the Giant's Leap. A giant is said to have jumped from it on to the top of Dunsinnan. A large boulder in the ravine used to be pointed out as one the giant tossed in the air when amusing himself.

Death at the Inn

Call in at the Sidlaw village of Rait on a sunny day in the month of July and you will not find a more peaceful or lovely spot. Yet it was on such a July day that a terrible murder once took place in the Rait inn.

The year was 1603 and the victim was John Sharp, servitor to the Laird of Ruthven. He had come to Rait to await the arrival of friends who were attending the funeral, in Perth, of the Laird of Ballindean (near Inchture).

In the village he was surprised to meet George Kinnaird, younger brother of the Laird of Kinnaird, and the Laird's son William, along with their friend, William Haitley of Balgavie.

He knew all three so when they invited him to join them for a drink at the inn he suspected nothing.

However, once they were seated in the tavern these three began to remonstrate with Sharp about an argument he had had with a friend of theirs, James Ramsay.

It turned out that Ramsay, too, was in the village that day.

'Let's send for him,' they said, and someone went off to fetch him.

Whether Sharp suspected anything or not is not known but he may well have grown uneasy as they awaited the arrival of the man he had quarrelled with just a few days before.

If he sensed danger, he was right to do so. Ramsay had no sooner entered the inn than he and the others unsheathed their swords and set about the unfortunate Sharp. He fell on the floor in a sea of blood from many wounds.

Ramsay took flight and seems to have disappeared. The two Kinnairds and Haitley were summoned to be tried for murder in November but failed to appear. They were declared to be outlaws but as time passed there was no sign of them being arrested and brought to justice.

The dead man's relatives made various efforts to have them brought to court and at last, in 1605, a trial date was fixed. This time it was the relatives who did not turn up. Someone had been working behind the scenes and a private agreement had been reached with the killers. The case was dropped.

The murderers of poor John Sharp went unpunished.

A Fiery Laird

Gasconhall sits on the south side of the Sidlaws between two burns, the Balmyre and the Rait. At the end of the sixteenth century it was owned by Robert Bruce of Clackmannan, a fiery individual who was to get himself in very hot water indeed through his explosive temper.

He first crossed swords with authority when his carrier was stopped by Customs officers in Perth when bringing goods to Gasconhall. Duty was demanded on the goods and they were to be held in custody until it was paid.

Bruce was livid. He sent word that his goods must be delivered to him at once or he would come and take them by force. Of course this threat was ignored.

Bruce took action: he attacked a group of Perth citizens returning along the Carse from Dundee and stole all their weapons. He then wrote to Customs in Perth offering to hand over the weapons if his goods were forwarded to him.

Next thing he knew a mob from Perth had descended on Gasconhall. They started to trample down his crops with their horses and do as much damage as they could. Bruce struck one of them a blow with his pistol and took two of them prisoner, locking them up in the house.

The others must have gone right back to Perth and complained to the Magistrates for that same night some of them arrived backed up with a number of supporters, including, one suspects, a few who were just looking for an excuse to cause trouble.

Fighting broke out, culminating in someone in the Perth party setting fire to Gasconhall. More than one person was injured in the blaze and Bruce himself was seized and dragged away while family silver and other possessions were looted.

Bruce was furious, and with good grounds, for all this had been done without legal authority. The matter went before the Privy Council who found that both parties, the Magistrates and Bruce, had broken the law.

Some of the Magistrates were imprisoned in Blackness Castle while the unfortunate Bruce was sent to cool off in a cell in Edinburgh Castle.

But he still had not learned his lesson. The very next year two Perth Councillors and others on their way to St Andrews Market were set upon at the Coble of Rhynd by Bruce and a group of armed men. Serious injuries were inflicted.

Bruce was summoned to appear before the King, failed to turn up and was declared to be a rebel.

Lucky Black Cat

The Kinlochs came over the Sidlaws from Dundee. They bought the estate of Balmyle in Strathmore and changed its name to their own.

One of several notable members of the family was Dr David Kinloch, Court Physician to James IV. The King had such a high opinion of his doctor that he often entrusted him with secret missions abroad.

On one occasion he sent him to Spain on delicate business. He came under suspicion from the authorities, was arrested and flung into prison.

The Inquisition was then in control, and one day the rumour reached Kinloch in his cell that the Grand Inquisitor had fallen ill and his Spanish doctors could not find a cure for him. Confident in his skills Kinloch asked the warders to send word that he would like to attend the patient. They just laughed at him.

He felt sure that if only the Inquisitor's attendants knew of his offer they would give him a chance. But how to get through to them?

He had only one friend in the prison—a black cat that used to come through his cell window to visit him. It was a beautiful animal, in prime condition, and so well groomed that Kinloch was sure it must belong to someone high up.

He scribbled a message and tied it to the cat's elegant tail. Off it went and he prayed that it would go straight home and that the piece of paper would not fall off on the way.

It must have survived the journey, for the next day his cell door was thrown open and he was led out and taken to the Grand Inquisitor's bedside. He soon saw what the trouble was, called for the appropriate medicines, and before long had the patient back on his feet.

As a reward honours were heaped on Kinloch, he was given a free pardon and, even more important, a safe conduct out of the country and back to Scotland.

He lies buried in The Howff, Dundee. The epitaph inscribed on the great stone reads as follows:

A most honourable man of famous learning and in his life adorned with singular virtues, a most skilled physician to the Kings of Great Britain and France, by whose patents and seals the antiquity of his pedigree and extract is clearly proven.

He scribbled a message and tied it to the cat's elegant tail…

The Fugitive

There was for long a tradition that Bonnie Prince Charlie, following Culloden, spent a night in hiding at Balthayock in the Sidlaw foothills. Historians dismiss this. It does not fit with what is known of his movements before he sailed for France. It could be that another fugitive from the battlefield took shelter there and the rumour grew that it had been the Prince.

At neighbouring Glendoick a more convincing story is told. Lord George Murray, the Prince's Lieutenant-General, is said to have hidden there for several days.

Murray, a son of the first Duke of Atholl, had thought long and hard before joining Charles's army at Perth. He had taken part in the 1715 Uprising and paid the price with several years in exile. Dare he risk everything again?

His Jacobite principles prevailed and he enlisted. It was to be a frustrating campaign for him. Although he was appointed Commanding Officer, Charles often disagreed with his advice and tactics. Lesser men, close to Charles, opposed his views.

Yet Murray was a soldier of genius. Had he been given full and undisputed control of his forces, the outcome of the Rising might have been dramatically different. There would have been no Culloden, for he foresaw the dangers of making a stand there and argued against it.

Now, for the second time in his life, he was a wanted man. At Glendoick friends provided him with a hiding place in the attic of a farm house. Only a select few knew that he was there, and he quickly learned to recognise the footsteps on the stair of everyone who came, in secret, to see him.

His stay there came to an abrupt and hasty end. One night he heard a strange step and then an unknown voice called out, 'Is Lord George Murray here?'

Thinking he had been discovered, Murray seized his sword and rushed down the stair shouting: 'I'll let you see Lord George Murray!'

He ran out through the door and disappeared into the darkness leaving the caller, whoever he was, behind him.

Murray did not return to the attic, and as day succeeded day and there was neither sign nor news of him, his friends began to fear that he had strayed into a nearby marsh, the Qua Loch, and been swallowed up by it. He would not have been the first traveller to disappear into one of its deep, dark holes.

Then, relief. Word came that he was safe and in France. From there he moved to Germany and then the Netherlands. He was never to see Scotland again.

Sir Gilbert's Revenge

In 1658 Sir Gilbert Hay, 10th Earl of Errol, married Lady Catherine Carnegie, daughter of the Earl of Southesk.

It looked like the perfect match, but it seems that the bride's father had doubts about his son-in-law from the start. He did not pay the tocher, the dowry due to his daughter when she wed.

Soon it was common knowledge that the couple's relationship was under strain. They were sleeping apart. As the months passed, the Earl of Southesk grew ever more determined not to hand over the customary money. This enraged Sir Gilbert and led to rows with his wife, which grew increasingly bitter as she took her father's side and accused her husband of being incapable of fathering a child.

Their intimate problems were aired in court in Edinburgh when she tried to win a divorce. The case was the talk of the town, much to the dismay of Catherine's sister, Jane, who was shocked and embarrassed by this washing of dirty linen in public. Rumours flew and some folk claimed that Catherine had tried to poison her husband, though there is no evidence to substantiate this.

As for Sir Gilbert he startled everybody by going off and taking a mistress, a pretty milkmaid, and setting her up in a room. This was no secret affair. He flaunted her openly, kissing and caressing her where they would be seen by people who knew him. He made sure Catherine saw them as well.

He proved her wrong, too, for the milkmaid became pregnant and bore him a son. Perhaps Sir Gilbert and his wife had simply been physically incompatible.

See a version of the ballad 'The Earl of Errol' later in the book (p.134).

Strife at Newtyle

For a time around the beginning of the eighteenth century two ministers were claiming the pulpit of Newtyle parish church. The church had been, like others, Episcopalian. Now things had changed and Presbyterian worship was the order of the day. The Rev. Alexander Mackenzie was the Episcopal priest who had been ousted. The charge had been given to a Presbyterian, the Rev. Mr Clephane.

The trouble was, Mackenzie refused to go. What is more, he had the personal backing of Bishop Halliburton then in residence at Hatton Castle, right on the kirk's doorstep.

Halliburton and Mackenzie enjoyed the support of many local people including some of the landowners. A number of villagers who would have attended Clephane's services were too afraid to do so.

Halliburton himself had been deprived of his position and authority, but that made no difference. There were few in the community bold enough to argue with him.

One Sunday Mr Clephane was making his way to conduct a service when he was confronted by a mob of 'armed hirelings'. He was forced to return to the manse.

The Episcopalians had learned that Clephane had publicly prayed in the kirk for King George and the Hanoverians. They sent him a stern letter warning him that if he did it again they would have him arrested and imprisoned in Perth.

Mackenzie took to holding services in a meeting-house, drawing larger crowds than Clephane in the church. Still, this was not enough for some of the hotheads. One day there was a hammering on the manse door. A band of Episcopalians burst in demanding to see Clephane. He was not there for he had gone into hiding; his wife and children could only look on, helpless, as the men rampaged through the house, smashing furniture and stabbing at the bedclothes, doing as much damage as possible. When they left they took family possessions with them.

It was no longer safe for Clephane to stay in the village. He spent some time abroad but when the unrest caused by the 1715 Uprising had died down and Presbyterianism was firmly back in the saddle Mackenzie had to admit defeat. He dropped his claim to the pulpit of Newtyle's church. Clephane returned and won back the sympathy and support of the parish. Mackenzie moved to Edinburgh where he died in 1722.

The Slave of Ballindean

Few people are aware that slavery in Scotland came to an abrupt end in 1778 thanks to the brave fight put up by an African purchased abroad and brought to work at Ballindean in the foothills of the Sidlaws in the Carse of Gowrie.

He was known as Joseph Knight, though that was not his real name. It had been taken from him along with his freedom and he had been renamed after Captain Knight, the slave trader who had brought him, in a hold crammed with many others, from his native Africa to Jamaica. Joseph was then about 12 years old, a frightened and bewildered boy.

He had been bought on the slave market by Sir John Wedderburn, later of Ballindean, then living in Jamaica. Sir John had a colourful past. His father had been executed in London in 1746 for taking part in the Uprising. Sir John had fought by his father's side at Culloden but when his father was captured he had managed to escape.

For a time he found shelter in the manse of Glenisla where the minister risked his own life by concealing him. He had even taken Wedderburn, disguised as a footman, to the General Assembly where no one suspected that 'John Thomson' was a member of a noble family and a hunted man.

Wedderburn slipped out of Scotland and went to America where he remained until the London Government passed an Indemnity Bill. He then went to Jamaica where he acquired wealth as a plantation owner, trader and medical man.

When he returned to Scotland in 1768 he brought his slave boy with him. Wedderburn had inherited several properties, and it was at this stage that he purchased the house and lands of Ballindean.

Joseph eventually married, and perhaps it was his wife who prompted him to seek his freedom. Whatever the circumstances, one day he simply walked out of Ballindean, not intending to return.

Sir John was furious. He had paid good money for Joseph and was not going to let him go as easily as that. Black servants were a considerable status symbol and he liked his guests to see Joseph about the place.

He reported Joseph for absconding, and before long he had been arrested and brought before Justices of the Peace. Joseph did not deny that he had walked out without permission but he defended himself vigorously, claiming that he was entitled to his liberty.

The Justices did not agree. They sided with Sir John and ordered Joseph to return to his service.

But Joseph was not prepared to give in. He appealed to the Sheriff of Perthshire, arguing that it was not right that he should be kept in slavery for the rest of his life. Sir John maintained that the bargain he had struck in Jamaica still stood and that he was entitled to retain Joseph's services for as long as he wanted them.

The Sheriff decided in Joseph's favour. He held that slavery was not recognised by law in this country and that the transaction in Jamaica had no validity here.

Sir John refused to accept the ruling. He insisted on an appeal to the Court of Session in Edinburgh. The case attracted a lot of attention and was hard fought on both sides.

For Sir John it was argued that he had acquired the legal right to Joseph's services throughout his lifetime; that he should not lose what had been his in Jamaica just because he had moved to Scotland. It was also argued that, if he was to be refused the right to Joseph's services in this country, then he could, if he wished, return him to Jamaica to work as a slave on the plantations.

Joseph must have wondered which fate would be worse: spending the rest of his life in forced service at Ballindean or being shipped back to the drudgery and hopelessness of the plantations.

On his behalf it was argued that Jamaican laws had no authority elsewhere and so the transaction Sir John had made was not recognised outside that country; slavery was unjust; Joseph had been a slave not by consent but by crime or conquest; the law which permitted slavery in Jamaica was patently unjust and could not be supported by the courts here.

As to returning him to Jamaica, this was based on the belief that one person could have complete dominion over another; this belief was false; Joseph was protected by a statute which prohibited the transporting of any person out of the country without his or her permission.

These were powerful arguments and they won the day, although the Lord President and three of the Law Lords dissented. The majority verdict was that: 'the dominion assumed over the negro under the law of Jamaica being unjust could not be supported in this country to any extent; that, therefore, the Defender had no right to the negro's services for a space of time, nor to send him out of the country against his consent, and that the negro was protected by Act 1701.'

Joseph Knight had won his fight for freedom. Not only that but, through his stand, he had killed off the employment of slaves in Scotland. If there were any other Josephs in stately homes across the country, they, too, from that moment, were entitled to be free men.

The Wife o' Denside

Her name was Mary Smith but for years after her trial, and long after her death, she was known as the Wife o' Denside. Street songs were written about her and she was spoken of with loathing. The name Denside gathered around it an aura of mystery and evil.

She was the wife of David Smith, the farmer at West Denside in the parish of Monikie, north of Broughty Ferry. He also ran the neighbouring farms of East Denside and Dodd, so the family was one of substance.

The Smiths had two sons, Alexander and George, two daughters and three female servants. One of the servants, Margaret Warden, had worked on other farms in the district since the age of 15 when her father had died leaving Mrs Warden to bring up two girls and a boy.

Mary Smith's sister, Mrs Machan, knew the Warden family and it was through her kindness that Margaret had been given a job at Denside.

Margaret was a lively, likeable lass and seems to have performed her duties well. She was popular with the young men on the farm and perhaps it was one of them who brought about her first misfortune. She fell pregnant and was sent home in disgrace to have the child under her mother's roof.

Mrs Smith was far from pleased, and that might have been the end of Margaret's employment at Denside had not Mrs Machan persuaded her sister to take her back. Again Margaret seems to have worked hard but, alas, her charms were once more to be her undoing. This time it was the Smiths' younger son, George, who fell for the vivacious servant lass.

He seems to have been genuinely fond of her, but as both knew that his parents would oppose the match they were forced to meet in secret.

It was from an interfering neighbour that Mrs Smith heard what was going on. At first she could scarcely believe it. She had high hopes for all her family and her plans for George did not include marriage to a servant who had already disgraced herself.

She kept watch and soon, with her own eyes, saw that the story was true: her son was meeting Margaret behind her back.

Of course she put all the blame on Margaret. She was nothing but a little schemer and George the innocent victim. She confronted the girl and lashed her with her tongue until Margaret ran from the house in tears.

Next morning she did not appear for work at Denside. Mrs Smith was going into Dundee with dairy produce, and as she had to pass the Wardens' cottage she stopped the coach outside and knocked at the door. It was Margaret who opened it.

What passed between the two at this meeting is not known. Mrs Warden was out but when she returned she was amazed to find Mary Smith trying to persuade Margaret to go with her to see a doctor.

At this time, the summer of 1826, typhus and cholera were rampant. Mrs Warden thought that Mrs Smith suspected Margaret might have caught one of these diseases. She assured her that the family had taken precautions against contracting them. However, Mrs Smith hinted darkly that it was something very different she feared.

As Mrs Warden saw her back to the coach she had to listen to a tirade against her daughter. Mrs Smith came out with it: she believed Margaret was pregnant again. 'If she is,' raged Mrs Smith, 'it will bring disgrace both upon you and me.' Her parting shot was that she was going to call on the doctor herself and would 'get something for Margaret'.

Shortly afterwards, harvesting began on West Denside. Margaret returned to help and was living in with the other servants. She soon found, however, that she was in no condition to tackle the strenuous work. To Ann, one of the servants, she confessed her pregnancy and admitted that George Smith was the father. In tears she told Ann that she would not be able to continue working much longer. She would have to leave Denside and implied that she would not be able to go home. She spoke despairingly of putting an end to herself.

As the girls sat at the side of the field Mrs Smith came over to them. Seeing Margaret's tears she spoke kindly to her and offered her refreshment from a flagon of tea. It was a small gesture but it was the first time Mrs Smith had shown her kindness and it gave Margaret a gleam of hope. Perhaps Mrs Smith was relenting and would, after all, accept her as a daughter-in-law.

Next day Ann noticed how much more cheerful Margaret was as she worked alongside her in the field. She toiled all day but when she returned to the servants' quarters in the evening she was very tired and fell into a doze before the kitchen fire. She was still sitting there at about 10 p.m. with another girl, Jean Norrie, when Mrs Smith came in with a large glass containing a whitish liquid.

She dipped a teaspoon into it and gave a sip of it to Jean, then handed the glass to Margaret and told her to drink the rest. Afterwards the two girls went to bed.

In the morning Margaret told Jean she was feeling sick and could not go to work. Jean went back to see her at lunchtime and found her still in bed. She was still there in the evening and was weak from vomiting.

Mrs Smith herself attended to the patient, showing concern and bringing her more tumblers of the whitish liquid telling her it was medicine and would help to cure her, but Margaret grew more and more ill. Her mother called to see her and was greatly alarmed.

Margaret had been taken ill on the Tuesday night. It was not until Friday that Mary Smith called in a doctor from Broughty Ferry. Before going in to see her he asked Mrs Smith if she had been giving her any medicine. 'Nothing but castor oil,' she replied. She asked Dr Taylor if he would be able to tell if Margaret was pregnant. He told her he probably could. She then asked if all the vomiting was likely to bring on a miscarriage, adding that if she gave birth 'it would be a stain on the family'.

Dr Taylor was, rightly, unwilling to discuss the matter and asked Mrs Smith to take him to the patient at once.

He found Margaret close to death. She was weak from the incessant vomiting and it was too late for him to do anything for her. A brief examination told him she was about three months pregnant. That evening she fell into a coma from which she never awoke.

Just two days after her death Margaret Warden was lowered into a grave in Murroes Kirkyard. Her only identification was a small plate screwed onto the coffin. It contained the minimum information, 'M.W., aged 25'. According to Dr Taylor's medical certificate she was just another cholera victim, so that seemed to be the end of the matter. It wasn't.

Margaret's sudden and violent illness had been the talk of the countryside. With her death, tongues wagged even more. It was common knowledge that she had been pregnant and everyone seemed to know who the father was and of Mrs Smith's antagonism towards the unfortunate girl. Lurid tales of the 'castor oil' she had been giving Margaret now abounded.

Someone brought the rumours to the attention of the Sheriff of Forfarshire, and after consultation, he made a dramatic decision: Margaret's body must be exhumed for examination.

It must have been one of the most grisly scenes ever to take place in an Angus churchyard. Dr Taylor was one of three doctors who witnessed the raising of the coffin. The lid was removed and the corpse—in an advanced state of decay—was laid on a large, flat gravestone. It was dissected there and then under the open sky. Parts of the stomach were removed and the body was then returned to the coffin, which was screwed down and restored to the grave.

The stomach contents, when analysed, proved that Margaret had not died of cholera but from arsenic poisoning. The rural community seethed with talk.

Mrs Smith was questioned on two occasions, the first at the Four-Mile House, Monifieth, and the second time in Dundee, by which stage she was being held in the city's Tolbooth. She insisted that it was castor oil that she had been giving the sick girl, but, under pressure, admitted that, not long before her death, she had bought rat poison for use on the farm.

She was charged with murder and a trial date was fixed for the end of December in the High Court, Edinburgh. In the event it did not take place until February 1827, having been postponed when one of the jury collapsed in an epileptic fit. Earlier postponements were made in order to give the defence time to trace witnesses they were anxious to bring forward, in particular a rat-catcher who had called at West Denside.

The defence case was that Margaret, in misery and despair over her unwanted pregnancy, had committed suicide by taking rat poison. They pointed out that there was not a scrap of evidence that Mrs Smith had given her anything more lethal than the castor oil she claimed.

On the other hand the prosecution called witnesses who swore there were few if any rats on the farm so why should Mrs Smith have bought a fresh supply if it was not for another purpose?

At last the jury was sent out to consider their verdict. The atmosphere in the court was electric when they filed back in and the tension was not broken when their decision was heard: 'Not Proven'!

A reading of the Lord Justice-Clerk's summing up of the case to the jury suggests that he considered Mary Smith guilty. When he now addressed the jury this view again comes through. Although he told them first that the Court was satisfied with 'the patience and attention' they had given to 'this extraordinary and very painful case', he then said: 'The verdict you have just returned… is *your* verdict, and I now discharge you from any other duty in the case.'

Turning to Mrs Smith and ordering her immediate release he said, 'I leave it to your own conscience before God, to apply their verdict in such a way as may be most conducive in this world, and to your eternal welfare hereafter.'

Barbed words indeed.

One cannot help but wonder, what were young George Smith's thoughts on the trial and the verdict? He was silent throughout the whole affair, yet had it not been for him none of it would have happened. Had he suspected his mother of poisoning Margaret? Did he care?

The verdict seems generally to have been greeted by the public with derision and contempt. The song-writers had a field day. It was the fashion at the time to write and publish songs and ballads dealing with current events. This version of 'The Wife O' Denside' was taken down in 1884 from the lips of a woman who had known Margaret Warden through working with her as a servant at West Denside. It was sung or recited on what was to be her deathbed to A.H. Millar, Dundee City Librarian, who subsquently wrote up the case for his historical series published under the title *Haunted Dundee* in 1923.

The Wife o' Denside

Ye'll a' hae heard tell o'
   The Wife o' Denside,
Ye've surely heard word o'
   The Wife o' Denside,
Wha pushioned her maid
   To keep up her pride,
An' the Deevil is sure o'
   The Wife o' Denside.

The Wife o' Denside,
   The little wee buddie,
She tried to tak up
   The trade o' the howdie,
But ah! ha, ha!
   Her skill was but sma',
For she pushioned baith lassie
   An' bairn an' a'.

Her tippet was brown
  An' her veil it was black,
An' three lang feathers
  Hung ower her back,
Wi' her purse by her side
  Fu' o' guineas sae free,
That saved her frae death
  At the Cross o' Dundee.

Oh, Jeffrey, Oh, Jeffrey,
  Ye hinna dune fair,
For ye've robbed the gallows
  O' its ain lawfu' fee,
An' it hadna been you
  An' your great muckle fee
She'd hae hung like a trout
  At the Cross o' Dundee!

Howdie—midwife
Francis Jeffrey—one of Mary Smith's two defence advocates.

On the Lighter Side

A Droll Lad

The Rev. Mason Inglis was once a guest preacher in a Sidlaw church where there was a very fussy beadle. Mr Inglis had been there before and he was always given the intimations with the admonition, 'An ye'll see and attend to that.'

This time it was no different, in fact Willie seemed even more concerned than usual that the single intimation be announced.

To make sure he did not forget, Mr Inglis gave it out at the start of the service. Unfortunately, Willie was still outside where he had been pulling the bell-rope. He had not heard the intimation so when, at the close of the service, Mr Inglis was launching on the benediction he was suddenly aware that Willie was half way up the pulpit steps.

'Whar is it?' he asked in a loud whisper. 'It's no made. It's no made ava!'

The congregation seem to have enjoyed the misunderstanding. One old elder laughed over it as he shook the minister's hand: 'Eh, but isn't he a droll lad, Willie?'

Name-calling

The minister of Auchterhouse and his neighbour at Tealing were good friends. One day the Auchterhouse man thought he would pull the other's leg. He said to him, 'It's a queer parish yours. If you put the letter S before it, Tealing becomes 'stealing'!'

His friend nodded. 'That is so, and if you put SL before Auchterhouse it becomes a much queerer parish, for it is converted into a 'slaughterhouse'!'

Falling Out

On one occasion these two worthies went to pay a call on a minister in Dundee. They rode there in a dog-cart. When he saw them off, their Dundee friend, knowing their propensity to argue, said, 'Now brethren, see that you don't fall out by the way.'

Next time they saw him they had to admit that they *had* fallen out. The horse had bolted and they had both landed on the road!

OLD CUSTOMS

Weddings and Wakes

As in other parts of the country, penny weddings were once very popular in Sidlaw communities. When a couple were to be married invitations were issued to all interested in coming. The penny they handed in on arrival went towards the food and drink.

As soon as the wedding ceremony was over the celebrations began. Ale and whisky flowed and music rang out from pipes and fiddles. The hilarity went on all through the night.

The Rev. Mason Inglis, minister of Auchterhouse at the end of the nineteenth century, says there were many attempts by ministers to put a stop to the penny waddins. These attempts were backed by the authority of the General Assembly but it took a long time before they began to die out.

He tells of a celebration that was held in a hut on 'a prominent spur of the Sidlaws'. One man was so delighted he was heard to exclaim, 'Weel, weel! If there's no been fun i' the Neuk the nicht!'

The place was afterwards known to locals as 'Funny-Neuk'. Where was 'Funny-Neuk'? I have searched the maps in vain.

Mr Inglis reminds us that wakes were another great excuse for knocking back the drams. When someone died, friends and relatives were invited to the house for 'the kistin' when the corpse was placed in the coffin.

Candles or lamps would be lit and the company would watch over the departed till morning with many a drink to while away the hours. Coffin-bearers at funerals were frequently the worse for wear. Not only would they be suffering from the effects of the night before but drink would sometimes be consumed at stages on the walk to the graveyard. The further they had to walk the worse their condition on arrival!

OLD RHYMES AND SAYINGS

When Craigowl has on his cowl
And Coolie Law his hude,
The folks o' Lundie may look dule
For the day will no be gude.

When Kinpurnie pits on her cowl
The weather will be wet and foul.

The Dean, the Dean, ilk seven years it taks ane and misses ane.

Mothers in Meigle would perform this dandling rhyme to the child on their knee:

This is the way the ladies ride,
Jimp and sma', jimp and sma';
This is the way the gentlemen ride,
Spurs an' a', spurs an' a';
This is the way the cadger rides,
Creels an' a', creels an' a'.
[at the gallop]
To Meigle, to Meigle, to buy a fat pig,
Home again, home again, jiggety jig!

Ane's nane, twa's same, three's a Curly Andrew.

(Curly Andrews, according to *Our Meigle Book*, were white 'curly-murly' sweets sold at Meigle Market).

In Strathmore, if someone was in trouble, he or she would be consoled with 'never mind, ye'll get ower this yet and into the big hoose o' Glamis.'

There are mair Mitchells than the Mitchells o' Meigle.

According to *Our Meigle Book* there were at one time many Mitchells, Michaels, Michaelsons and Mitchelsons in Meigle district and, further back, Gillemichaels.

This is the way the ladies ride,
Jimp and sma', jimp and sma';
This is the way the gentlemen ride,
Spurs an' a', spurs an' a'…

Someone or something of great age would be described as being 'As auld as the Moss o' Meigle'. The Moss has long since been reclaimed.

❧

This verse was collected from a ploughman in the Carse of Gowrie. Tinkletap, in the Carse, is one of several places in Scotland bearing the name.

> When plooin sair at Tinkletap
> I tore my breeks upon a prap;
> I tied them up wi binder twine
> An cairried on till lousin-time.

❧

> The fowk o' Pitroddie
> Cam doon the fit-roadie,
> And stealt a' ma peas,
> Coddie for coddie;
> Gin I catch them again
> I'll gar a' their heids
> Play needletie noddie!

❧

> Grace and peace cam by Collace
> And by the doors o' Dron;
> But the Cauple-Stowp o' Abernyte
> Maks mony a merry man.

(The Cauple-Stoup was an inn owned by a character known as 'Auld Bowkie'. However, another version of the rhyme has it, 'But the caup and stoup o' Abernyte mak mony a merry man.')

❧

> The muckle pat o' Abernyte,
> The jordan o' Inchture, O,
> The bonnie bells o' Forgan,
> And Rossie riggs sae dear, O.

(A 'pat' is a pot and a 'jordan' a chamber-pot so you can make what you like of this one!)

❧

> High on its hill, a bonnie hill,
> Stands Kinnaird Kirk in Gowrie;
> To ane and a' its bell does ca'
> 'Come worship God in Gowrie'.

❧

A Strathmore mother would sing this rhyme to the baby on her knee:

Ridin on a horsie,
Never standin still
Doon by St Martin's an ower by Newmill,
In by the Guildtown an roon by Cargill,
Richt by Burntbrae and ower by Gallowhill,
Yont by the Harelaw an doon tae Wolfhill,
An *that's* the wey tae ride a horse
An never stand still!

Between Sidlaw and the sea
Pest or plague shall never be.
(Old prophecy)

On the Lighter Side

Bearing Up

A ploughman cycling home along the Carse of Gowrie in the early hours of the morning was once startled to see a bear rise up in front of him from the ditch at the side of the road. He rushed into his house, grabbed his gun, and ran out and shot it dead.

Next moment a furious figure was berating him. He was a Frenchman and he had been sleeping in the ditch. The animal had been his performing bear. Now his means of livelihood was gone.

The ploughman was brought to Court but discharged. There was a lot of local sympathy for him, but even more for the Frenchman. A public subscription was raised to buy another bear.

A song was written about the incident. It was based on the popular music hall song of the time 'The Man Who Broke the Bank at Monte Carlo'. The new version was called 'The Man Who Shot the Bear in the Carse o' Gowrie'.

The Leear

The Sidlaws have long attracted geologists. During the course of a Geological Survey of Scotland the eminent Professor James Geikie climbed Evelick Hill in the company of a Mr Morrison of Murie.

Morrison later told what happened. It was a sunny day and he had rested on the grassy summit while Geikie went off to examine the rocks. A shepherd had appeared and Geikie, in talking to him, had started to explain how the hills had been formed. He told him of volcanoes in Fife, the crack which had extended from the sea westwards and much more. He was an enthusiast and was eloquent in his description.

When the shepherd moved off he met Morrison who asked him if he had seen his friend.

'Is he a lad wi a straw hat and checkit troosers?'

'Yes, that's him.'

The shepherd looked at him earnestly. 'He's an awfy leear, yon man!'

A Wheen o' Witches

The Witch of Cardean

At Cardean, near Meigle, about 200 years ago, lived a woman called Jean whom everybody believed to be a witch. She lived alone in a cottage by the river Dean, close to a thick wood.

Although local folk were a little afraid of her they were always ready enough to seek her help. If any farmer had a sick animal he would ask Jean to take a look at it. She could nearly always cure it and she made no secret of where she learned her skills. She would boast that she had been taught them by Auld Nick himsel'.

One day she received an urgent request from a farmer who wanted her to come as quickly as possible to a cow that was dying. His farm was some miles away and, to save time, she left the track and cut across a field. The farmer saw the figure crossing his land and shouted to her that she had no right to be there. To his fury she took no notice but carried on her way.

He hurried and caught up with her, then ordered her to turn back.

Coldly she looked him up and down. 'Do you ken who I am?' she asked.

'No—and I don't care!'

'I am the Witch-wife of Cardean,' she said. 'And if you don't tak yourself off quickly I'll mak you die where you stand!'

The man turned pale with fear. He had never seen her before but he knew her reputation.

'Go on your way,' he muttered. 'I have nothing more to say to you.'

And he let her pass.

She was often called in to settle arguments and on one occasion a woman walked all the way from Forfar with a companion to seek her advice about belongings that had been stolen from her.

Jean's methods were inclined to be strange. This time she began by asking them each to eat a tallow candle, wick and all. Then she questioned them both. So shrewd were her questions that the woman's companion suddenly broke down and confessed that it was she who had stolen the items from her friend.

The Witch-wife used often to go out into the woods at night not returning till morning when she would emerge covered with scratches and bruises. She was not afraid to let it be known that she had been quarrelling with her Master, the Deil, and they had come to blows.

However there came a night when she went out and did not return. As time passed the villagers became concerned. They went in search of her and found her body floating in the Dean. So ended the mysterious life of the Witch of Cardean.

Warlock Mungo

A woman living in the Carse was unlucky enough to have a male witch as a neighbour. Every night Warlock Mungo, as he was called, used to come into her house to ask the time.

One night he walked in with his hands hidden behind his back, under his coat-tails. When he pulled them out she saw he was holding a bridle. He repeated some strange words and she was turned into a mare.

He jumped on her back and made her fly through the air. They flew across the sea and then overland until they came down in Bordeaux in France. There he tethered her outside a doorway and went inside. She could do nothing until he came out, unhitched her and made her fly home again.

Next morning the woman's friends were worried when there was no sign of her about the house. They went in and found her still asleep, exhausted after her night's journeyings.

She never let Warlock Mungo over her door again.

Jenny the Witch

Jenny Gairie was the cause of a lot of trouble in her day. She lived on the old Moor o' Forgan and her witchcraft made her feared for miles around.

Robbie Curr's uncle was one of those who suffered from her spells. His horses and cattle were dropping dead one after another and he was certain it was her work.

He was brooding on this one day as he made his way to Dundee and he grew more and more angry as he thought about her. So when he saw her ahead of him walking on the road he pulled up his horse and drew out his knife.

He leaped to the ground and threatened her with it, swearing he would kill her if she would not promise never to harm another of his beasts.

Jenny could see he was a desperate man. There was murder in his eyes. Maybe, too, she felt just a wee bit sorry for him. Whatever the reason, she gave him a piece of advice.

'Let me alone,' said she, 'and I'll tell ye whit to dae so that neither I nor ony ither witch can touch your beasts.'

'Weel,' said the man. 'Tell me!'

'Get yoursel a white cock. That'll dae it.'

Robbie's uncle looked at her doubtfully, but after a moment's hesitation he put his knife away, remounted his horse and rode on to Dundee. When he came home that night he had with him a white cock. Soon it was strutting the farmyard, lord of the flock. And not one of the farm beasts came to any more harm through witchcraft.

That was not the first time Robbie's uncle had encountered Jenny Gairie on the road to Dundee. On a previous occasion he had been riding on a cartload of hay. Three times the cart couped over for no apparent reason. The third time he saw a mouse run out from amongst the hay where it had fallen on the road.

The mouse scuttled into the ditch and Robbie's uncle chased after it. When he looked through the long grasses into the ditch there sat Jenny under a briar grinning up at him.

She could turn into other creatures too. There were times when local men had been hunting a hare and it had run in at her door. When they looked inside they saw no hare but only Jenny, back in human form.

She had a daughter, Mary, of whom she was very proud. A young man called Jamie Walker fell in love with her and she felt the same about him.

Jenny knew they were courting and she did not approve. She didn't want Jamie as a son-in-law. One day when he was calling to see Mary, Jenny invited him in and offered him a drink in a black cup. He drank it and was a simpleton for the rest of his life.

When Jenny died at her home at Powgavie there were sighs of relief all over the district. Still, they gave her a decent funeral. Her coffin was placed on spokes and carried from the house to the graveyard in the traditional manner. They said that as they carried it up the brae one of the spokes broke and a hare came running down the road and ran right underneath the coffin.

The Shod Wife

Robbie Curr, the Carse storyteller, had several tales of witches in that area. One took place on a farm which was owned by a widow. She had a son and they employed two men.

The two ploughmen lived in a bothy where they shared the same bed. For some time one of them had been waking up in the morning feeling more tired than when he lay down. He told his bedmate about it saying his nights were always restless. He kept dreaming he was flying through the air. In the mornings he could hardly drag himself to yoke the horses.

The other man listened carefully and then told him he had sometimes wakened during the night and seen his friend was not there. Tonight, he said, we'll change places. I'll sleep on your side of the bed.

That night the man who had been having the bad dreams fell straight into a deep sleep. The other kept awake. About midnight the door softly opened and in came the widow. Through half-closed eyes he saw that she held a bridle in her hand. She shook it over his head and said some words. At once he turned into a horse.

She led him out, leaped on his back and rode off. He found himself flying through the night sky. They travelled a long way, and when at last she guided him down to earth they were in Italy. There she tethered him by a doorway and went inside.

As soon as she was gone he started to rub his head against the wall and push at the bridle with one of his hooves until he succeeded in slipping it off. In an instant he was a man again.

He picked up the bridle and waited by the doorway. When she came out he shook the bridle over her head and repeated the words he had heard her say over the bed. She vanished and a mare stood in her place. He jumped on her back and took up the reins, saying, 'Ye gied me a gey heat comin awa, but I'll gar ye pey for it gangin hame!'

Off she flew into the sky and they sped through the darkness under the stars. By the time they arrived back in the farmyard the mare was white with froth as though they had come through a snowstorm. He dismounted and tied the bridle firmly to her head, then led her into the stable where he tethered her to a stall. Then he returned to bed, where the other man was still enjoying a dreamless sleep.

At daybreak, leaving him still sleeping peacefully, the ploughman rose and went to find the widow's son.

'I've a fine mare for sale,' he told him. 'I think you should buy her.'

'I'll need to see her first,' said the son.

'Ye'll soon see her for she's in the stable.'

The son followed him to the stable and had a good look at the mare. After he had examined her all over—her teeth, her legs, her hooves—he said, 'She's a bonny mare richt enough. Braw and fat. Whaur did ye get her?'

'It disna maitter whaur I got her, but she's no stolen, dinna think that. Noo, it must be cash doon for I'm needin the money.'

'But hoo much are ye wanting for her?' asked the son. 'Her mooth tells me she's no very young and there's anither thing—her front hooves are awfu flat.'

'That's nithing,' said the ploughman. 'Her feet just need shoein. If you say aicht pound, she's yours.'

The farmer hesitated. 'Will ye promise me she's a guid worker?'

'I canna say aboot working but for ridin she baits a' the beasts I ever had a leg ower!'

'My mither's no at hame,' said the son. 'I dinna ken whaur she is or I'd ask her whit she thought.' He scratched his head. 'I'll gie ye six pound and tak my chance.'

Just then the other ploughman came along, having wakened up from his deep sleep. He, too, inspected the mare and advised a compromise. 'Mak it seevin,' he suggested.

The two men agreed and the son paid on the spot.

All three took the mare to the smiddy at Rait to have her shod. She was restive and wouldn't stand still but the smith was a strong man. He seized her and held her in a tight grip. Well he knew there was always a good dram for him when he shod a horse for the first time. The mare was helpless in his powerful hands. Soon she had four fine shoes on her feet.

The son was a proud man as he led her home. There was no doubt about it, the mare was a handsome animal. He looked forward to showing her off to his mother when she returned.

He led her into the stable, put her in a stall and took off the bridle. Flash! The mare had gone and there sitting in the stall was his mother glaring at him with

She vanished and a mare stood in her place…

horseshoes on her hands and feet. The two ploughmen thought they had never seen anything so comical. They laughed at the indignant expression on her face and at the son's amazement when he found the mare he had paid for was his own mother.

Robbie Curr used to finish this tale by telling his listeners that he remembered the son's bairns. 'I kent them brawly,' he would say. 'They were aye ca'd the Shod-Wife's owes' (grandchildren).

On the Lighter Side

The Cook's Story

John Fraser was cook for the family at Duntrune, north of Broughty Ferry, for 60 years, serving three generations of owners. He was described by the writer Dean Ramsay as 'a waggish old man' and here is an example of his humour.

He had sent to the dinner table a roast goose which looked perfect except that one leg was missing. His master suspected that John or someone else in the kitchen had taken it and he sent for John and demanded an explanation.

'Och,' said John, 'Dae ye no ken that a' the geese roond here hae but ae leg? Juist look!' He pointed through the window to where a flock of geese were standing sleeping—all of them perched on one leg.

The Laird looked at the geese, then back at John. He arose, opened the window, clapped his hands and cried 'Whew!' The geese lowered their other legs and flew off. He turned to John who said, 'Noo if you had cried "Whew!" tae the ane on the table it wad hae done the verra same!'

A Little Further

Andrew Bonar came as a minister to Collace in 1838. A few months later one of his parishioners, a farmer, met him early on the road and said, 'Ye'll be gaun tae Perth the day, Mr Bonar?'

'No,' replied Bonar. 'I'm going to Jerusalem!'

And so he was for he had been chosen by the General Assembly to go there on a Mission of Enquiry.

Tales of the Track

The Railway Age

Many strange sights have been seen in and around the Sidlaws: however one of the most extraordinary had nothing of the supernatural about it but had everything to do with industrial expansion and the desire to accumulate wealth.

It happened on the railway line that, in the face of enormous geographical difficulties, was built to run through the hills and provide a link between Dundee and Newtyle.

Despite the obvious physical problems the Dundee and Newtyle Railway Company attracted over 150 shareholders, including such eminent names as the Earl of Airlie, Lord Wharncliffe and the politician George Kinloch. Charles Landale, an engineer and the son of a Strathmartine millowner, and James Carmichael of the Ward Foundry in Dundee, were both heavily involved in the enterprise.

It all took shape in the early 1800s when industrial Dundee was rapidly expanding. The roads to the north were poor and an alternative means of transporting goods was seen as vital.

In Strathmore, landowners also recognised the advantages: the line could carry farm and garden produce to the crowded streets of the city and bring back supplies to country dwellers. Newtyle could be developed as a spinning and weaving centre with the imported raw materials brought to it cheaply and quickly.

The original idea had been even more ambitious and unlikely. In 1817 the Magistrates of Dundee had considered the construction of a canal between the city and Strathmore. Around the same time, at the other end of the Sidlaws, thought was being given to a canal leading northwards from Arbroath.

Both ideas were dropped and the plans for a rail line to Newtyle were placed before Parliament and approved in 1826.

Charles Landale had undertaken to chart a route for the track to Strathmore. He came up with a choice of two. Both followed the same route from Dundee as far as Strathmartine. From there one would run by the Kirkton of Auchterhouse and Balbeuchly to Newtyle while the other swung north-east to Tealing and entered the strath at Douglastown.

The first was considered the better option, and work on construction began. The promoters gave themselves a huge obstacle right at the start when they sited the Dundee station in Ward Road. Immediately behind it rose a steep hill. The only way to get the train up there was by a stationary steam engine. Near the top a tunnel had to be burrowed through a shoulder of the Law to allow the line to reach the flat lands of Downfield and Strathmartine. It was easy going across these until the Balbeuchly Incline where another stationary engine was needed. A third was required to haul the train over Hatton Hill.

To begin with the train consisted of just a single coach. There was no engine and it had no power. When it was not being hauled up the hills by the ropes of the stationary engines it had to be pulled by horses, first across Strathmartine to the foot of the Sidlaws and then, once over Balbeuchly, along to the Glack of Newtyle. It then trundled happily down the hill to its village terminus.

A strange sight the 'train' must have made as it proceeded in stately fashion behind its horse across the countryside. It must have been one of the only railways in the world ever to use a sail. William Whitelaw, the horse driver, made one out of waggon cloth and when the wind was right he hoisted it on a pole above the carriage. He then unhitched the horse and trotted along behind keeping an eye on his charge. If the wind dropped he would take down the sail and hitch up the horse again.

The coach itself was very simple. It was the body of an old stagecoach, minus its wheels. This primitive contraption made her maiden journey on 16 December 1831. The operating company had already encountered unexpected problems. Parts of the Law tunnel had collapsed, causing several fatalities. Costs of land purchase and the laying of the track had been higher than forecast. More money had to be borrowed to complete it.

Still the promoters persevered. In 1833 steam locomotives replaced the horse and sail. The 'Earl of Airlie' and 'Lord Wharncliffe', named after two of the most powerful proponents of the enterprise, were built in Dundee by J. and C. Carmichael. New coaches were purchased so that passengers might travel in a more dignified manner. Instead of a single journey each day, as had been the case to start with, there were now three or four.

Goods traffic increased. Much of it reflected the rural nature of the line: potatoes, grain, manure and lime. But there was also coal, iron, flax, stone and slate. The stones and slates were for the streets of tenements being built to house the mill and factory workers of burgeoning Dundee.

There were high hopes that the line would be a commercial success and its progress was watched closely in other areas of Britain. The contemporary railway and canal historian Joseph Priestley wrote that he saw it as: 'Very important to the mountainous (!) district of country through which it passes, affording access to the port of Dundee which hitherto seemed quite impracticable.'

Improvements were made in attempts to increase its use. It had always been the hope, especially on Landale's part, to extend the line deep into Strathmore. This was done in 1837 when the railway reached Coupar Angus, thanks to a new company, the Newtyle and Coupar Angus Railway Company (motto 'Time Is Precious'). Glamis, too, was connected up.

At the Dundee end, the steep haul up the Law from Bell Street was abandoned and a new route laid from the Harbour to Ninewells and round the back of Balgay Hill. A wider loop between the Dighty Burn and Auchterhouse cut out the Balbeuchly Incline, and an embankment approaching the Glack of Newtyle replaced the old route along the edge of the Sidlaws.

Despite all this, the Dundee-Newtyle Railway failed to become the success and fortune-creator of its promoters' dreams. Newtyle did not grow into a hive of industry. Passenger traffic remained light—it was never going to be anything else in so thinly populated a countryside. The journey time of one hour between Dundee and Newtyle was an improvement on the old coach service but there was just not enough demand for it.

The company's shareholders reaped no dividends on their investment, and in 1846 the Dundee and Newtyle Railway Company leased the line to the Dundee and Perth Railway Company.

A branch line from Coupar Angus to Blairgowrie was opened in 1855 and brought fresh passenger and goods business. Several Dundee businessmen built houses in Blairgowrie and were amongst the first commuters, travelling daily to their desks in the city and returning in the evenings to their rural retreats. In the early 1900s trainloads of rasps, fresh from the Berryfields o' Blair, started their journey south at Blairgowrie Station.

The passenger service on the Dundee-Newtyle line survived until 1955 and it closed down completely eleven years later when the track was taken up. The Blairgowrie branch failed by just a few months to reach its centenary.

Had Newtyle developed as a planned industrial village, the story could have been very different. It was thought at one time that there might be several such centres across Strathmore. Kirkinch was to be one of them. Washington was to be another. Its story is told by Christopher Dingwall in his excellent *Ardler—A Village History: The Planned Railway Village of Washington*. He explains how handloom weaving, which it was intended to develop in places such as Newtyle and Washington, was killed off by the new power-looms. The mills of Dundee and the Ericht at Blairgowrie and Rattray came to dominate the area's textile trade.

The brave new world of Washington (named after the first US president) simply petered out. Even the name Washington slipped out of use. There is still a Washington House and a 'Washie Brae', but the older name of Ardler is the one that prevails.

Travellers' Joys

As was to be expected the Dundee-Newtyle Railway was, in its early years, a great wonder to all who saw or used it. When the first locomotive was to make its maiden journey from the city, an old Auchmithie fisherman walked all the way to Dundee and climbed the Law to watch.

On his return to Auchmithie he told his friends, 'It puffed an' it puffed, an' it cam and it cam, and when it saw me it ran into a hole an' hoded!' (hid).

Prior to the introduction of the locomotives, the stationary engines gave endless trouble. The ropes that were wound round them kept breaking, sending the train slipping backwards.

They sometimes snapped when the train was travelling downhill as well. A country woman was aboard one day when the rope broke on the hill going down to the Ward Road terminus.

She was taking butter and, worse, eggs, to sell in the town and when the train rushed headlong into the station and came to a sudden halt, she was flung out on to the platform and her produce scattered.

As she gathered herself together and surveyed the damage she exclaimed, 'Oh, sirs, I likit the ride but they hae sic a rough wey o' coupin' fowk oot I dinna think I'll gang back wi' it!'

Another woman, thrown to the floor when the rope snapped going down to Newtyle, got out and enquired, 'Is this Newtyle then? They micht hae a cannier wey o' settin' fowk doon!'

A Blairgowrie man breathed a sigh of relief when the train reached Lochee. 'I think I'm by the warst noo,' he said to a fellow-passenger.

'Why—where are you going?' asked the passenger.

'Cape Town!'

A woman who had travelled from Dundee was challenged at Newtyle for not having bought a ticket for her son who was obviously over age for free travel.

'Och,' she retorted, 'ye maun mind he's a growin' laddie and this is a gey slow train!'

Travelling on the line could be dangerous even on the flat stretches. The converted stagecoaches that served as carriages were far from ideal, as this official warning shows: 'Although passengers on the outside have a fine view of the countryside, they are in great peril when approaching bridges.' Ouch!

The history of the line is strewn with accidents and near-disasters. Tragedy struck at Newtyle when a farm labourer stepped behind the train. It ran backwards and killed him. A woman died on one of the occasions when the winding rope snapped.

Even as late as 1929 passengers could still be at risk. About six o'clock one January evening a coach was being shunted at Newtyle when it ran away and proceeded through Alyth Junction and up the Alyth branch to Jordanstone.

An Alyth man, John Younger, was in the coach and he recalled the event years later in the *Dundee Courier*. He remembered it was pitch dark which made the experience all the more frightening. 'There was a fair bit of panic in the coach because of the speed we were travelling and one lady had to be restrained from jumping out of the door.'

The coach slowed to a stop at the gradient at Jordanstone but then started to run back the way. It did so for about a mile before finally halting.

Mr Younger was a daily traveller between Jordanstone and Lochee, and despite this hair-raising misadventure he said he was not deterred from using the line and took his seat as usual the next morning.

The signalman at Newtyle Junction on the night of the incident was Alexander Bell, later of Bankfoot. He wrote to the *Courier* to tell what he remembered about it:

'I got the emergency runaway signal (four bells followed by five and five) from the Newtyle Station box. I then had to make a split-second decision as to whether to send the runaway along the main line to Ardler or on to the Alyth branch. I chose the Alyth Branch, but no one thought the coach would ever run as far as it did. We thought it would be stopped by a light hump near Meigle.'

He recalled that an enquiry into the mishap was held next day in, of all places, the waiting room at Alyth Junction. It was found that the cause of the runaway was a broken brake rod.

As a commercial enterprise the Dundee-Newtyle Railway was a failure. It was, however, a brave and ambitious enterprise and as Scotland's very first passenger line it is a part of world rail history. The vision of a line that would surmount the natural obstacle of the Sidlaws was a bold one as was the idea that it would service a group of industrial pockets in Strathmore.

Traces of the line can still be seen and the route can be followed, with diversions where a bridge has disappeared or houses built. As we negotiate the roads in the area today with their increasingly fast and unpredictable traffic, it is hard not to feel more than a little envious of the passengers who sat in state in these coaches of yesterday and watched the world slip by at a leisurely pace. The carriages were maybe never the last word in comfort or safety, but who, sitting behind the wheel of a car now, would not change places with their passengers?

The Iron Horse

The building of the railway between Dundee and Perth must have been as great a 'ferlie' for the people along the Carse as the one that crossed the Sidlaws from Dundee to Newtyle.

In his comic song 'The Iron Horse', Charles Balfour puts himself in the shoes of a yokel venturing to travel by train for the very first time and bewildered by the whole experience.

Balfour was ideally placed to observe the reactions of passengers for he was stationmaster at Glencarse. He is said to have sworn that there was at least one passenger who believed that the entire Dundee station was to be transported to Perth and that he did not need to board the train!

He put his words to the tune 'Smith's a Gallant Fireman' and first sang it in public at 'a festival of railway servants' in 1848. The song became highly popular in Dundee, Perth and the villages of the Carse. It also appealed to the bothy singers of the north-east.

In the 1960s I recorded a fine version sung by Charlie Lamb, the Dundee folksinger, while my friend Peter Shepheard collected an equally good one from the Fife singer, Eck Harley. Both tunes, and the words of Eck's version, are in Nigel Gatherer's *Songs and Ballads of Dundee* (1986).

This earlier version is from 1893 when it appeared in *The Harp of Perthshire* edited by Robert Ford.

Come Hieland man, come Lowland man, come every man on earth, man,
And I'll tell you how I got on atween Dundee and Perth, man;
I gaed upon an iron road, a rail they did her ca', man;
It was ruggit wi an iron horse, an awfu beast to draw, man.
    Sing fal lal la.

Then first and foremost, near the door, there was a wee bit wicket,
It was there they gar'd me pay my ride, and they gied me a ticket,
I gaed awa up through the house, sat down upon a kist, man.
To tak a look o' a' I saw on the great big iron beast, man.

There was hooses in a lang straught raw, a' stannin upon wheels, man;
And then the chiels that fed the horse were as black's a pair o' deils, man;
An the ne'er a thing they ga'e the brute but only coals to eat, man—
He was the queerest beast that e'er I saw, for he had wheels for feet, man.

A chap cam up, an round his cap he wore a yellow band, man;
He bad me gang an tak my seat. Says I, 'I'd rather stand, man.'
He speer'd if I was gaun to Perth. Says I, 'an that I be, man;
But I'm weel enough just whaur I am, because I want to see, man.'

He said I was the greatest fule that e'er he saw on earth, man;
For it was just the hooses on the wheels that gaed frae this to Perth, man.
An then he laught an wondered hoo I hadna mair discernment,
Says I, 'the ne'er a ken kent I; I thought the hale concern went.'

The beast it roared, an aff we gaed, through water, earth, and stanes, man;
We ran at sic a fearfu rate, I thought we'd brak our banes, man;
Till by and by we stoppit at a place ca'd something Gowrie,
But ne'er a word had I to say, but only sit an glower aye.

Then after that we made a halt, an in comes yellow band, man;
He asked me for the ticket, an I a' my pouches fand, man,
But ne'er a ticket I cud get—I'd tint it on the road, man—
So he gar'd me pay for't ower again, or else gang aff to quod, man.

Then after that we crossed the Tay, an landit into Perth, man,
I vow it was the queerest place that e'er I saw on earth, man,
For the hooses an the iron horse were far aboon the land, man,
And hoo they got them up the stair I canna understand, man.

But noo I'm safely landit, an my feet are on the sod, man;
When I gang to Dundee again I'll tak anither road, man;
Though I should tramp upon my feet till I'm no fit to stand, man,
Catch me again when I'm ta'en in wi a chap in a yellow band, man.

The tiny train that ran on the Inchture branch line is described in these verses:

> It was but ae railway carriage
> Divided intae twa,
> The ae end was for common folk,
> The other for the braw.
>
> For engine was an auld gray horse
> That ran between the rails,
> And pu'd alang the passengers,
> The luggage and the mails.

The Dundee–Newtyle Railway

(Song)

> If you wad leave Dundee behind
> I'll tell ye what t'dae,
> Just tak the railway frae Ward Road
> That rins tae the tap o' the brae
>   On the railway line.
>
> It leaves the pubs and dens behind,
> The Overgate as well,
> You'll feel a younger man by far
> When you get the country smell
>   On the railway line.
>
> It stops at Downfield Station syne
> And noo the air is sweet,
> Strathmertine's howe is a bonny sicht
> Tae a man frae a Dundee street,
>   On the railway line.
>
> Twas here a dragon aince was kill't
> Or so the auld fowk say,
> Gin they be peek'n oot the noo
> They'll think he's alive the day,
>   On the railway line!
>
> Oh, there's a ferm and there's a hoose
> And noo we're at Rosemill,
> It's here the engine gies a shak
> And maks for the Seedlee Hills
>   On the railway line!

Barbeuchly's stey, Barbeuchly's lang,
Barbeuchly's hard tae gain,
There's times ye feel ye'll slip right back
Tae the fit o' the hill again
    On the railway line,

But syne we're up on Hatton Hill,
We've traivelled mony a mile,
An noo its doon like a hoody craw
Tae the village o' Newtyle
    On the railway line!

Maurice Fleming

Two Ghosts

The Kilspindie Ghost

What happened to the Hustons of Kilspindie Castle? What calamity overcame the castle itself? Charles Spence, the mason poet who lived in the neighbouring village of Rait, wrote a ballad which told the following extraordinary ghost story.

The young Laird of Kilspindie wooed and won a beautiful girl. We will call her Lady Margaret and him Edward.

Poor Margaret soon realised that to her husband she was nothing more than an ornament, a possession that meant less to him than his horse, his hounds and his hawk. Hunting was his passion and he would ride off at dawn, returning weary and mud-stained as darkness fell. It was no different when their child was born. Edward saw less of his son than he did of his favourite horse.

Margaret, knowing she was not loved, grew increasingly sad and lonely. She spent her days wandering on the hill slopes behind Kilspindie, often sitting by the waters of one of the little burns that rose higher up and flowed down to the flat lands of the Carse.

One warm summer evening she was resting in a shady glade overlooking a little waterfall, listening to the song its waters played. Her page was sitting nearby when he was suddenly startled to glimpse a small grim face peering at Lady Margaret from a yew tree close to where she sat. As the page watched, transfixed, the little man drew a green wand and waved it over her, muttering a spell.

Margaret slipped into a deep sleep and the little man melted into the branches of the yew. The page ran forward and tried to wake his mistress. When he touched her hand she was icy cold. No amount of rubbing would warm it and nothing would rouse her.

He sped back to the castle to raise the alarm. Soon he was leading a party to where he had left her by the waterfall. But when they burst into the clearing it was empty. All that night they searched and for days afterwards, up the glens and into every nook and hidden corner of the hills. No trace of her was to be found. She had vanished from the face of the earth.

Edward, her husband, joined half-heartedly in the first searches, but he soon lost interest and returned to his old ways, spending his days hunting far and wide over the countryside.

It was some time later, on a cold, moon-washed night, that Lady Margaret returned. As midnight struck, the watchman inside the castle door was startled by a knock. It worried him because he had heard no approaching footsteps, no rattle of harness.

'Who's calling so late?' he demanded from behind the closed door. 'I'm not letting you in at this time of night.'

A woman's voice replied, soft and low. 'I can come in without your leave—and go out again.'

Next moment a shadow seemed to pass in front of him, so faint he wasn't sure if he had seen one. Then a hand, light but cold as death, touched his.

'Go and rest,' said the voice. 'It's no night for keeping vigil here.'

He knew that voice well.

'Lady Huston!' he gasped. Shaking with fear he began to apologise for his rudeness. He could not see her but he knew she was there, in front of him.

'Where is my child?' murmured the voice. 'I have come to see him.'

The man told her he was with the nurse.

'And my husband? I hope he is asleep for I do not want to meet him.'

'He will be asleep,' said the man. 'You won't waken him. He will be dreaming of his horse and his hounds. He goes hunting the stag tomorrow.' The man paused, and then burst out, 'Oh, my Lady, he never loved you. It was a lonely life you led.'

Again there was that light, cold touch on his hand.

'Tell no one what has happened tonight. Now, please lead me to my son.'

He picked up his lantern and led the way up stairs and along corridors. There was no sound behind him but he knew Lady Margaret was following. He could sense her presence at his shoulder.

At last he stopped outside a door. 'This is the room. Your child is in there.'

There was no need to open the door. In an instant Lady Margaret was bending over her sleeping son and then lifting him to cradle him in her arms. She kissed him over and over.

In a corner of the room the nursemaid stirred in her sleep but did not waken. Had she done so she would have seen a small elfin figure appear.

'Come,' said the little figure. 'We must go now.'

Lady Margaret laid her baby gently back in his cot. A few minutes later a pale shadow flitted through the closed front door of the castle and melted into the night.

Edward Huston knew nothing of all this when, in the morning, he rose and put on his hunting clothes. He was in jovial mood as he tugged on his boots. It was a fine morning, the sun was rising and he looked forward to a great day at the chase.

He smiled as he heard the hounds baying in front of the castle, eager to be off. His friends awaited him and his horse would be saddled and ready. Humming, he clumped downstairs to be greeted respectfully by his servants. He climbed into the saddle, the signal was given for the huntsman to sound his horn and, with shouts of glee, the party proceeded at a good pace up into the hills.

The thrill of the hunt… There was nothing like it for Edward Huston. To be galloping over rough country in pursuit of a stag was for him the greatest delight on earth. That day was as good a day's hunting as he had ever known. One beast after another was pursued and pulled to the ground by the hounds.

They were chasing another, the biggest and noblest yet, when a strange thing happened. Edward's horse stopped short and would go no further. In vain he whipped and cajoled it. His friends, not noticing, had galloped on out of sight. He was left alone in a secluded dell.

As his horse reared and bucked, suddenly there before him stood Margaret, dressed from head to toe in green. She approached and stroked the horse's muzzle, calming it with a quiet word.

'Edward,' she said, 'would you save our love? I am under a spell, but it can be broken. I know how to do it but it needs your help. It is our last chance.'

'Spell!' spluttered Edward. 'What nonsense is this?'

She told him how a spell had been cast over her. There was only one way it could be broken—through love. 'I could love you again as I once did, but you would have to love me.'

He shook his head. 'I don't believe a word of this. It's plain to me that you ran off with someone else. Now he has tired of you and you want me to take you back. Well, I'm not doing it!'

She looked up at him sorrowfully. 'Then I can never return. It is all over. But because of your lack of trust in me, you will put your trust in a sword and it will break that trust. Not for three generations will good fortune again smile on Kilspindie.'

Slowly the figure in green faded and disappeared.

'Margaret!' he shouted, but she was gone.

For a time after that the Laird of Kilspindie was a worried man. As the years passed, however, he pushed all thoughts of his bewitched wife to the back of his mind, pretending it had never happened.

He died in battle, swinging his sword against a foe he should easily have felled. At the crucial moment his sword went weak in his hand. He remembered Margaret's words as he fell to his death.

The once proud castle of Kilspindie became a gloomy place, falling into ruin. If Lady Margaret ever visited it again I cannot say, though there are stories that her green figure has been seen wandering on the hills behind the castle.

A family of children living in a lonely house in the Sidlaws used to say that a strange lady sometimes joined them. She would weave daisy chains for the girls and with rushes she made shields and helmets for the boys. Then they played what she called the Fairy Game. Afterwards she would slip away as quietly and mysteriously as she had come.

Perhaps she is still there in the deeper recesses of the Sidlaws behind ill-fated Kilspindie.

The White Lady

North of Longforgan, just off the A85 with its relentless traffic, lies the little village of Benvie on the Invergowrie Burn. The people here were once very troubled by the ghost of a lady in white. At nights she wandered up and down the burnside weeping, wailing and wringing her hands.

It was very distressing for everybody and at last they went to their minister and asked him, 'Can you not do something about it?'

So in the middle of the night he rose, donned his robes, took up his Bible and made his way in the moonlight to the banks of the burn. For a time all was quiet except for the call of an owl and the scuffle of tiny creatures in the grasses.

Then he heard it. Her cries reached him long before she did. Along the bank she came, her dress gleaming white in the moonlight. He stepped in front of her and she stared, surprised. Until now everyone had avoided her. Quietly he asked her, what was the matter? Why was she so sad?

In a voice heavy with grief she told him she was the spirit of a woman who had died of the Plague. Because she had been a stranger to the district she had been buried in unconsecrated ground. There would be no rest for her until her body was dug up and placed in a grave in hallowed soil.

If this was done, she promised, a spring would rise from the grave, the waters of which would be a cure for the Plague for all time.

Next morning the minister told all the villagers what she had said. Fortunately someone remembered a strange woman dying and the place where she had been buried. He led the men to the spot and the body was recovered. A new grave was dug in the churchyard and everyone gathered round while the minister read the burial service.

From that hour the White Lady of Benvie was heard and seen no more and, as she had promised, a well sprang up, the waters of which were a cure for sufferers from the Plague.

LEGENDS OF GLAMIS

Castle of Tales

Visit Glamis Castle on a bright summer's day and you come away with the impression of a happy, smiling place. The welcome at the door is warm, the guides are pleasant and entertaining, the café lively. You may not meet or even glimpse the family who live here, but you sense they are there and that they love and cherish their home.

And what a home! With that great, imposing frontage and forest of towers, it is not surprising Glamis has become one of the best-known buildings in Scotland. Many folk who have never been there carry an image of it in their mind.

Some people, when they think of Glamis, will think of Elizabeth, the Queen Mother, who, as Elizabeth Bowes-Lyon, spent part of childhood here. Others will remember those terrible scenes from Shakespeare's *Macbeth*... Lady Macbeth urging her husband to kill old Duncan, the sleepwalking scene, the guilt, anguish and terror.

It's all lies, of course. Or rather, artistic licence. Duncan died, a young man, in battle. Macbeth and his wife were not a pair of ogres but a well-liked king and queen.

Still, the story clings to the walls of Glamis and will as long as Shakespeare is read and performed.

Other stories are told of this amazing building, some of them perhaps less easy to dismiss, for as the castle has grown and spread over the centuries, metamorphising from the simplest beginnings to what we see today, so tales have grown with it and linger on, sinister shadows behind the smiles and the polite well-rehearsed tours.

The Fairy Hill

The earliest tale takes us back many hundreds of years and tells why the castle does not stand on the site originally chosen for it. It should have been built on Denoon Law three miles away.

According to the legend, Denoon was an ancient home of the fairies, a place they regarded as their own. When, one day, they saw the first workers climb the hill and begin to dig foundations for a building, they were outraged. To aid them in their resistance, they sought help from a company of demons or evil spirits who were the sworn enemies of mankind.

The demons were delighted with the chance to foil the plans of the builders. At dead of night, after the workmen had gone home, a swarm of demons landed on the hill. In the morning the workmen were astonished to find the foundations destroyed.

They started work again, and this time the demons waited till the walls had risen some way off the ground. Then they struck again. The walls were tumbled to the foot of the Law.

The head builder responded by taking on more and better workmen. He thought that if he could build the walls more quickly and make them stronger, whoever was pulling them down would be defeated and would give up.

The men worked hard and the walls rose thick and solid, but the demons still managed to push them over and hurl the stones to the foot of the hill.

The builder was mystified. Who was doing this? He determined to find out. After a long day during which the men dragged up the stones and once again set them one on top of another, he sent them home as usual, but he waited behind and hid to watch what would happen.

For a long time all was silent, then in the middle of the night he heard a rushing sound. A demon came flying towards the Law on the wind. As it passed over his head it cried out:

> 'Build not on this enchanted ground,
> 'Tis sacred all these hills around;
> Go build the Castle in a bog
> Where it will neither shake nor shog!'

After that, a new site was chosen and Glamis Castle arose on the flat ground it occupies today while the fairies lived on at Denoon Law undisturbed.

Archaeologists tell us that an early fort once occupied the summit of Denoon. The story of its rise and fall, and the men who occupied it, is long since forgotten—or does the tale of the fairies and demons contain some faint echo of events from the distant past?

The Mysteries of Glamis

One night in the nineteenth century, a lady staying at the castle awoke to see a huge man with a great beard sitting apparently asleep in front of the fire. From the description she gave it could have been the ghost of the notorious 'Earl Beardie', but if it was he was enjoying a rare moment of repose.

'Beardie' was the fourth Earl of Crawford, a larger-than-life character, and he came to grief here when he came to the castle for a game of cards with Lord Glamis and several other gentlemen. Well into the night a terrible quarrel arose. Glamis accused Beardie of cheating and pushed him out of the room and down the stairs. Beardie came back in shouting and swearing and demanding that the game should continue. Everybody refused to return to the table, terrified of this great raging giant.

'Alright,' he roared, 'if none of you will give me a game, I'll play with the Devil himself till Doomsday!'

At that a tall dark stranger nobody had noticed before stepped forward and said he would play cards with Beardie. The two sat down, the stranger dealt the cards and they began to play. According to the legend, they are at it still. The room was closed off from the rest of the building so that they could continue, and more than one person claims to have heard Beardie as he sits there, shouting and banging on the table, condemned out of his own mouth to play for all time against an opponent he can never defeat.

That tradition is public knowledge, as is the one that Glamis Castle contains a secret room and that its location and the grim tale behind it have been passed down by each head of the family to the next, all sworn to secrecy. I have been told that someone with access to the castle once counted all the windows inside and then from outside and that there was one more outside than there should have been.

The story told is that an heir to the family was born hideously deformed, that a report was put out that the baby had died when, in fact, it was put into the secret room and kept locked up there for the duration of its life, which was a considerable number of years.

But even if that were true, why should the room still be kept a dark secret? Might it be because it contains the skeletal remains of 'The Monster' or other evidence of his existence? Successive Earls of Strathmore and Kinghorn have declined to discuss the matter—perhaps because it is only a story and there is nothing to discuss.

There is another tale told of an Earl opening the door to a room he had never looked in before and seeing the floor littered with skeletons. He fainted, and when he recovered he relocked the door and never went back.

The remains were said to have been those of a party of Ogilvys who were being pursued by some Lindsays with whom they had a feud. The Ogilvys arrived at the castle door and pleaded with the Earl to give them protection. He took them in, led them to a room in a remote part of the building and locked them in. No one heard their cries and screams for help and they died in an agony of starvation and thirst. It is said their cries and groans may still be heard if you venture along a certain corridor.

About the middle of the nineteenth century a group of workmen were repairing the floor of a room in the castle when they came on a stone spiral staircase hidden within the solid walls. They suspected this might lead to the famous secret room but did not dare to investigate.

Apart from Beardie's ghost—if it is his that has been seen—there are said to be others. Little seems to have been recorded of the White Lady, but there is a Grey Lady who haunts the chapel and has been seen a number of times, at least once by the Dowager Countess Granville, a sister of Elizabeth the Queen Mother.

She said she was sitting playing the organ one day when she had an odd feeling there was someone else present. She turned round and saw a little woman in a grey dress kneeling in prayer in one of the pews. The sun shone right through her.

Another harmless ghost is that of a black pageboy who has been seen sitting patiently waiting outside the door of a certain room.

A much more unpleasant apparition is that of the Tongueless Woman. Her terrible story is as follows:

A guest staying at the Castle was strolling in the grounds one evening when he glanced up and saw a white, terrified face looking down at him from a window. The poor woman seemed to be in great distress and he went closer. Even as he did so, she uttered a scream and was pulled back out of sight.

Not knowing what to do he waited and presently saw a door open below the window. An evil-looking old crone came out, carrying a heavy sack on her back. She scuttled off with it into the woods. He had a horrible suspicion the sack contained the woman he had seen at the window.

Some years later, on a walking holiday in the Italian Alps, he sought shelter from a storm in a monastery. One of the monks told him that a woman from his own country was cared for in a nearby nunnery. She had, he said, been a servant in a big household and had stumbled on a secret they were desperate to keep quiet. So that she could never tell it to anyone, or even write it down, they had her tongue cut out and her hands chopped off. She was then sent to spend the rest of her days in this remote mountain nunnery.

The man asked if he might be allowed to see her. He was led through the snow to the other building and taken to a dim room where the woman sat. Peering at her in the half-light he gave an exclamation. It was the woman who had stared at him from the Glamis window.

Since King Duncan did not die at Glamis, there is no fear of his ghost lurking around. The King who did die within these walls was his grandfather, Malcolm II. There is a tradition that he was murdered in the castle and that his assassins drowned trying to cross the ice on Forfar Loch as they made their escape. When the loch thawed, their bodies were fished out and hung on gibbets by the wayside.

Another school of thought says that, although he died in the castle, it was from wounds received in a skirmish at Hunter's Hill nearby.

Malcolm deserves to be remembered because it was during his reign that the Scotland we know today took recognisable shape. He was succeeded on the throne by Duncan who was to die at the hands of Macbeth.

The Grey Lady who haunts the chapel may be Jane who was married to the 6th Lord Glamis (or Glammis as it used to be spelled). She was a member of the Douglas family whom James V suspected of plotting against him, which, in fact, they were. When the 6th Lord died, Lady Jane married again, this time a Highlander called Campbell. He was arrested along with her, her sixteen-year-old son by Lord Glamis, and an elderly priest.

The accusation of witchcraft was made against her but the real charge was one of attempting to poison the King and of being in league with her two rebel brothers.

Throughout her trial in Edinburgh she had the sympathy of the people. She is said to have been very beautiful and to have conducted herself with a quiet and impressive dignity. Even when she was condemned to be burned at the stake, she remained serene and went calmly to her death.

The next day her husband, Campbell, tried to escape from his cell in Edinburgh

Castle by climbing down a rope lowered from the window. The rope was too short and he fell to his death.

The old priest was released but Lady Jane's son was kept in captivity for five years. He was then freed, had his lands and title restored, and returned to Glamis as the 7th Lord.

If the Grey Lady who kneels in prayer in the chapel is Lady Jane, it does not sound as if she will be praying to be forgiven for anything she did against the King. Perhaps what disturbs her spirit is that, through her activities, her husband met an early death and her son lost the best years of his youth.

Most of the stories told of Glamis Castle are very old, but here is one that is said to have happened only last century. It concerns a man who was staying at the castle as a guest of the Earl of Strathmore.

One night he lay in bed unable to sleep. Restless, he rose and went to the window. His room was at the front of the castle, the grounds were bathed in moonlight, and at the far end of the avenue he saw something moving. It drew closer and he realised it was a carriage coming up the drive. The strange thing was that as it drew nearer he realised it was making no sound. He could see the wheels turning but no noise reached his ears.

The silent carriage stopped at the entrance below him, there was a short pause, and then it set off again. As it wheeled round the driver glanced up at him with a disfigured and terrible face. Horrified, the man watched the carriage roll off down the drive as silently as it had come.

He slept little for the rest of the night and in the morning when he went down to breakfast he said to the Earl, 'You had a very late arrival last night.'

'No,' said the Earl, 'there was no arrival.'

'But I saw a carriage drive up.'

The Earl turned pale and said nothing. When he spoke again it was to change the subject.

The guest left Glamis without mentioning what he had seen again. Not long afterwards he was in Paris. At the end of a tiring day he returned to his hotel room and dressed for dinner.

His room was on the third floor and he decided to take the lift down to the restaurant on ground level. He pressed the bell and the lift appeared. There were several people in it and they made room for him, but just as he was about to enter the liftman raised his head and looked at him. It was the terrible face he had seen at Glamis.

He stepped back, the doors closed and seconds later there was a great crash.

The lift had collapsed and everyone in it was dead.

Whatever you do, don't be put off by these strange and even grisly tales. Glamis Castle is a delightful place to visit and you will soon forget them as you proceed from one beautiful room to another. There is much to admire, much to be learned, and it is, without doubt, one of the best-preserved of the great houses open to visitors in Scotland. I strongly recommend it—ghosts or no ghosts!

Ballads, Songs and Poems

Sir James the Rose

O heard ye o' Sir James the Rose,
    The young heir o' Baleichan?
For he has killed a gallant squire,
    Whase friends are out to tak him.

Now he is gane to the house o' Mar
    Whaur nane might seek to find him;
To see his dear he did repair,
    Weining she would befriend him.

'Whaur are ye gaun, Sir James?' she said,
    'O whaur awa are ye riding?'
'I maun be bound to a foreign land,
    And now I'm under hiding.

'Whaur shall I gae, whaur shall I run,
    Whaur shall I rin to lay me?
For I hae killed a gallant squire,
    And his friends seek to slay me.'

'O gae ye doon to yon laigh hoose,
    I shall pay there your lawing,
And as I am your leman true,
    I'll meet you at the dawing.'

'I'll no gae doon to yon laigh hoose,
    For you to pay my lawing,
But I'll lie doon upon the bent,
    And bide there till the dawing.'

He's turned him richt and round about
    And rowed him in his brechan,★
And laid him doon to tak a sleep
    In the lawlands o' Baleichan.

★ plaid

He wasna weel gane out o' sight,
  Nor was he past Milstrethen,
When four-and-twenty belted knights
  Cam riding owre the Lethan.

'O hae ye seen Sir James the Rose,
  The young heir o' Baleichan?
For he has killed a gallant squire,
  And we are sent to tak him.'

'Yes, I hae seen Sir James,' she said,
  'He passed by here on Monday;
Gin the steed be swift that he rides on,
  He's passed the Hichts o' Lundie.'

But as wi' speed they rade awa,
  She loudly cried behind them,
'Gin ye'll gie me a worthy meid,
  I'll tell ye whaur to find him.'

'O tell, fair maid, and on our band,
  Ye'se get his purse and brechan.'
'He's in the bank aboon the mill,
  In the lawlands o' Baleichan.'

They sought the bank aboon the mill,
  In the lawlands o' Baleichan,
And there they found Sir James the Rose,
  Lying sleeping in his brechan.

Then out and spak Sir John the Graeme,
  Wha had the charge in keeping,
'It's ne'er be said, my stalwart feres,
  We killed a man when sleeping.'

They seized his braid sword and his targe,
  And closely him surrounded,
And when he waked out o' his sleep,
  His senses were confounded.

'Rise up, rise up, Sir James,' he said,
  'Rise up since now we've found ye;
We've ta'en the braid sword frae your side,
  And angry men are round ye.'

'O pardon, pardon, gentlemen,
    Hae mercy now upon me!'
'Such as you gave, such shall you have,
    And so we fall upon thee.'

'Donald, my man, wait till I fa',
    And ye shall hae my brechan,
Ye'll get my purse, though fu' o' gowd,
    To tak me to Loch Lagan.'

Syne they took out his bleeding heart,
    And set it on a spear, O,
They took it to the house o' Mar
    And showed it to his dear, O.

'We couldna gie ye Sir James' purse,
    Nor yet could we his brechan,
But ye shall hae the bluidy heart,
    O' the young heir o' Baleichan.'

'Sir James the Rose, O, for thy sake
    My heart is now a-breaking;
Cursed be the day I wrocht thy wae,
    Thou brave heir o' Baleichan!'

Then up she raise, and forth she gaes,
    And in that hour o' tein, O,
She wandered to the dowie glen,
    And never mair was seen, O.

The Earl of Errol

O Errol's place is a bonny place,
    It stands upon yon plain;
The flowers on it grow red and white,
    The apples red and green.

The ranting o't and the danting o't,
    According as ye ken,
The thing they ca the danting o't,
    Lady Errol lies her lane.

O Errol's place is a bonny place,
    It stands upon yon plain;
But what's the use of Errol's place?
    He's no like other men.

'As I cam in by yon canal,
    And by yon bowling-green,
I might hae pleased the best Carnegie
    That ever bore that name.

'As sure's your name is Kate Carnegie,
    And mine is Gibbie Hay,
I'll gar your father sell his land,
    Your tocher for to pay.'

'To gar my father sell his land,
    Would it not be a sin,
To give it to a naughtless lord
    That couldna get a son?'

Now she is on to Edinburgh,
    For to try the law,
And Errol he has followed her,
    His manhood for to shaw.

Then out it spake her sister,
    Whose name was Lady Jane;
'Had I been Lady Errol,' she says,
    'Or come of sic a clan,
I would not in this public way
    Have shamed my own gudeman.'

But Errol got it in his will
    To choice a maid himsel,
And he has taen a country-girl,
    Came in her milk to sell.

He took her by the milk-white hand,
    And led her up the green,
And twenty times he kissed her there,
    Before his lady's een.

He took her by the milk-white hand,
    And led her up the stair;

Says, 'thrice three hundred pounds I'll gie
    To you to bear an heir.'

He kept her there into a room
    Three quarters of a year,
And when the three quarters were out
    A braw young son she bear.

'Tak hame your daughter, Carnegie,
    And put her to a man,
For Errol he cannot please her,
    Nor any of his men.'

Archie o' Kilspindie

Wae worth the heart that can be glad,
    Wae worth the tear that winna fa',
For justice is fleemyt frae the land,
    An the faith o' auld times is clean awa'.

Our nobles they hae sworn an aith,
    An' they gart our young king swear the same,
That as lang as the crown was on on his head,
    He wad speak to nane o' the Douglas name.

An wasna this a wearifu' aith;
    For the crown frae his head had been tint an gane
Gin the Douglas' hand hadna held it on,
    When anither to help him there was nane.

An the king frae that day grew dowie an wae,
    For he liked in his heart the Douglas weel;
For his foster-brither was Jamie o' Parkhead,
    An Archy o' Kilspindie was his Grey-Steil.

But Jamie was banisht an Archy baith,
    An they lived lang, lang ayont the sea,
Till a' had forgotten them but the king!
    An he whiles said, wi a watery e'e—
'Gin they think on me as I think on them,
    I wat their life is but drearie.'

It chanced he rode wi hound an horn
　　To hunt the dun an the red-deer down,
An wi him there was mony a gallant earl
　　An laird, an knight, an bold baron.

But nane was wi him wad ever compare
　　Wi the Douglas so proud in tower and town,
That were courtliest all in tower and hall,
　　And the highest ever in renown.

It was dawn when the hunters sounded the horn,
　　By Stirling's walls, so fair to see;
But the sun was far gaen down i' the west
　　When they brittled the deer on Torwood-lee.

An wi jovial din they rode hame to the town
　　Where Snawdon★ tower stands dark an hie;
Frae least to best they were plyin the jest,
　　An the laugh was gaun round right merrily.

When Murray cried loud, 'Wha's yon I see?
　　Like a Douglas he looks, baith dark and grim;
And for a' his sad and weary pace,
　　Like them he's richt stark o' arm and limb.'

The king's heart lap, and he shouted wi glee—
　　'Yon stalwart makedon★★ I ken richt weel;
And I'se wad in pawn the hawk on my han'
　　It's Archy Kilspindie, my ain Grey-Steil;
We maun gie him grace o' a' his race,
　　For Kilspindie was trusty aye, an leal.'

But Lindsay spak in waefu mood
　　'Alas! My liege, that mauna be.'
And stout Kilmaurs cries, 'He that daurs,
　　Is a traitor to his ain countrie.'

And Glencairn, that aye was doure and stern,
　　Says, 'Where's the aith ye sware to me?
Gin ye speak to a man o' the Douglas clan,
　　A gray groat for thy crown and thee.'

When Kilspindie took haud o' the king's bridle reins,
　　He louted low down on his knee;

★Old name for Stirling　　★★ Stout body

The king a word he durstna speak,
    But he looked on him richt wistfullie.

He thought on days that lang were gane,
    Till his heart was yearnin and like to brast;
As he turned him round, his barons frowned;
    But Lindsay was dichtin his een fu fast.

When he saw their looks, his proud heart rose,
    An he tried to speak richt hauchtillie—
'Gae tak my bridle frae that auld man's grip;
    What sorrow gars him haud it sae sickerlie?'

And he spurred his horse wi gallant speed,
    But Archy followed him manfullie,
And, though cased in steel frae shoulder to heel,
    He was first o' a' his companie.

As they passed, he sat down on a stane in the yett,
    For a' his grey hair there was nae ither biel;
The king staid the hindmost o' the train
    And he aft looked back to his auld Grey-Steil.

Archy wi grief was quite fordone,
    An his arm fell weak that was ance like airn,
An he sought for some cauld water to drink,
    But they durstna for that doure Glencairn.

When this was tauld to our gracious king,
    A red-wud furious man woxe he,
He has ta'en the mazer cup in his hand,
    And in flinders he has gart it flee—
'Had I kent my Grey-Steil wanted a drink,
    He should hae had o' the red wine free.'

And fu sad at the table he sat him down,
    And he spak but ae word at the dine—
'O I wish my warst fae were but a king,
    Wi as cruel counsellours as mine.'

John Finlay

Castle Guthrie

The Angus houses of Guthrie and Brigton were eventually united with the marriage of a Laird of Guthrie to Anne Douglas of Brigton, but in earlier times there was an unhappier episode as this ballad relates:

In plume and doublet rides the knight,
　　On a summer morning early,
Of noble bearing, comely face,
　　His steed cap'risoned rarely.

And loud he knocks at Brigton's gates,
　　The warder asking sternly:
'From whence come you?'—Sir David cries,
　　'I come from Castle Guthrie.

Go quickly tell your lady fair,
　　I would see her thus early,
I to the tournament away,
　　And cannot longer tarry.'

The lady looks from her lattice high,
　　Her lover gazing fondly:
'The Guthrie would the Douglas wed?
　　Back hie to Castle Guthrie.

Aside your tilting trappings throw,
　　Your armour buckle fairly,
The wars! The wars! Haste to the fray,
　　Then having suffered sairly,
And won your spurs by noble deeds,
　　You ever fighting bravely,
Come back and claim your willing bride—
　　Then ho! for Castle Guthrie!'

Forth to the wars Sir David went,
　　His pride and love taxed sorely,
The foremost ever in the fight,
　　His spurs he won right bravely.
Now homeward speeds he proud in haste
　　To claim his bride right fairly,
Upon her own conditions won—
　　All hail to Castle Guthrie!

'What sounds are these in Brigton's halls,
    Of revelry thus early?'
''Tis e'en our Lady's nuptial day,'
    Leered the warder glibly.

In haste again Sir David sped
    To the wars now raging fiercely—
In battle slain, ne'er saw again
    His own loved Castle Guthrie!

The following rhyme records the properties once all in Guthrie hands:

Guthrie of Guthrie,
    And Guthrie of Gaigie,
Guthrie of Taybank,
    And Guthrie of Craigie.

Ye'll Mount, Gudeman

Lady
'Ye'll mount, gudeman; ye'll mount and ride;
Ye'll cross the burn, syne doun the loch side,
Then up 'mang the hills, thro' the muir and the heather
And join great Argyle where loyal men gather.'

Laird
'Indeed, honest luckie, I think ye're no blate,
To bid loyal men gang ony sic gate;
For I'm gaun to fecht for true loyaltie,
Had the Prince ne'er anither, he still will hae me.'

Lady
'About Charlie Stuart we ne'er could agree;
But dearie, for aince, be counsell'd by me;
Tak' nae pairt at a'; bide quietly at hame,
And ne'er heed a Campbell, M'Donald, or Graham.'

Laird
'Na, na, gudewife, for that winna do,
My Prince is in need, his friends they are few;
I aye lo'ed the Stuarts: I'll join them the day:
Sae gie me my boots, for my boots I will hae.'

Lady

'Oh! saftly, gudeman, I think ye're gane mad;
I hae na the heart to preen on your cockaud;
The Prince, as ye ca' him, will never succeed;
Ye'll lose your estate, and maybe your head.'

Laird

'Come, cheer ye, my dear, and dry up your tears!
I hae my hopes, and I hae my fears;
But I'll raise my men, and a' that is given,
To aid the gude cause—then leave it to Heaven.

'But, haste ye now, haste ye, for I maun be gaun,
The mare's at the yett, the bugle is blawn,
Gie me my bonnet, it's far in the day,
I'm no for a dish, there's nae time to stay.'

Lady

'Oh, dear! Tak' but ane, it may do ye gude!'
But what ails the woman? She surely is mad!
She's lifted the kettle, but somehow it coup'd
On the legs o' the laird, wha roared and louped.

Laird

'I'm brint! I'm brint! How cam it this way?
I fear I'll no ride for mony a day!
Send aff the men, and to Prince Charlie say,
My heart is wi him, but I'm tied by the tae.'
The wily wife fleeched, and the laird didna see,
The smile on her cheek thro' the tear in her e'e—
'Had I kent the gudeman wad hae had siccan pain,
The kettle, for me, sud hae coupit its lane!'

Lady Nairne

❧

The Lass o' Gowrie

'Twas on a summer's afternoon,
A wee before the sun gaed doon,
A lassie wi a braw new gown
   Cam ower the hills to Gowrie.
The rosebud wet wi morning shower
Blooms fresh within the sunny bower,

But Katie was the fairest flower
 That ever bloomed in Gowrie.

I praised her beauty loud and lang;
Around her waist my arms I flang,
And said, 'My dearie, will ye gang
 To see the Carse o' Gowrie?
I'll tak ye to my father's ha
In yon green field beside the shaw;
I'll mak ye lady o' them a—
 The brawest wife in Gowrie.'

Saft kisses on her lips I laid;
The blush upon her cheek soon spread:
She whispered modestly and said—
 'I'll gang wi you to Gowrie.'
The auld folks soon gae their consent;
Syne to Mess John we quickly went,
Wha tied us to our hearts' content;
 And now she's Lady Gowrie.

Anonymous

According to Robert Ford in his anthology, *The Harp Of Perthshire*, there are at least four versions of the song 'The Lass o' Gowrie'. The following one is by Lady Nairne.

'Twas on a summer's afternoon,
A wee before the sun gaed doon,
A lassie wi a braw new goun
 Cam ower the hills to Gowrie.
The rosebud wash'd in summer's shower,
Bloom'd fresh within the sunny bower;
But Kitty was the fairest flower
 That e'er was seen in Gowrie.

To see her cousin she came there,
An oh! the scene was passing fair;
For what in Scotland can compare
 Wi the Carse o' Gowrie:
The sun was setting on the Tay,
The blue hills melting into grey,
The mavis and the blackbird's lay
 Were sweetly heard in Gowrie.

Oh, lang the lassie I had wooed
An truth an constancy had vowed
But cam nae speed wi her I lo'ed,
    Until she saw fair Gowrie.
I pointed to my faither's ha',
Yon bonnie bield ayont the shaw,
Sae lown that there nae blast could blaw,—
    Wad she no bide in Gowrie?

Her faither was baith glad an wae;
Her mither she wad naething say;
The bairnies thocht they wad get play,
    If Kitty gaed to Gowrie.
She whiles did smile, she whiles did greet;
The blush an tear were on her cheek—
She naething said, an hung her head,
    But now she's Leddy Gowrie.

Hey the Rantin Murray's Ha'

Murrayshall, east of New Scone, has for some years been a popular hotel. Lady Nairne's song suggests it has always been renowned for its hospitality, but who was Peggy and what became of her? She leaves the mystery hanging and 'the ghaist in the wa'.'

Hey the rantin Murray's Ha'!
Mirth and glee amang them a'!
The country laird, the lady braw,
They'll welcome ye to Murray's Ha.
Come ye hungry, come ye dry,
Nane wad ever need to wait;
Come ye brisk, or come ye shy,
They'll meet ye or ye're at the gate.

Some were feasting in the Ha',
Some at sports upon the green,
Peggy, flower amang them a',
Dancin like a Fairy Queen.
Blithest o' my blithest days
I hae spent at Murray's Ha',
But oh, my heart was like to break
When I saw Peggy gang awa.

Whaur she gaed or why gaed she,
Few were there that weel could tell;
I thought it was to lightie me—
She maybe scarcely kenned hersel.
They said a ghaist was in the wa',
Sometimes aneath, sometimes aboon;
A'body heard—naebody saw,
But a' were sure they'd see it soon.

Some say the General, honest man,
That feared nae bullets, great or sma',
Wad rather face the Mons Meg gun
Than meet the ghaist o' Murray's Ha'.
Tis no the gate, I think ava,
To lay a ghaist wi' mirth and glee;
Scholared lads and lasses braw
Need nae ghaist or goblin dree.

The General referred to was Thomas Graham, Lord Lynedoch (1748-1843), hero of Corunna, Barossa and other battles. His estates were near Methven, but he was related to the Murrays of Murrayshall and visited them there. The Murray family erected a tall monument to him on Murrayshall Hill.

The Laird o' the Lonzies

This song by Charles Spence can be sung to the tune 'The Laird of Cockpen'. The placename is often spelled 'Longies' or 'Longeis' but the spelling here is the one used by James M. Strachan in his collected works of Spence, *From The Braes of the Carse* (1898). Mr Strachan was minister of Kilspindie and Rait.

According to Melville in *The Fair Land of Gowrie* the lands of Lonzies were near Evelick Castle 'at the foot of the brae, about midway between the ancient villages of Kilspindie and Rait'. Lonzies House, he states, stood to the west of the crossroads at the bottom of the Rait Brae. The estate disappeared when it was added to the lands of Rait.

The Laird o' the Lonzies was forty years auld
When his daddy was laid i' the vault damp and cauld;
And when he had mourned for a year and a day
He coost off the black coat and put on the grey.

Ae gloamin when walkin aboon Ferrie Knowes
Wi' his cousin, and talkin o' horses and cows,
Quoth she to the Laird, 'At your time o' life
It is strange you're no thinkin o' takin a wife.

The lands o' the Lonzies for five hunder years
Hae aye been possessed by your worthy forbears,
But afore they were forty they always took care
That the lands o' the Lonzies should not lack an heir.'

Quoth the Laird, 'Ye hae spoken sense aince i' your life;
For sax ooks I've been thinkin o' takin a wife:
Douce Margret our milkmaid, a thriftier lass
Ne'er scougied a cog, nor ca'd kye frae the grass.

She makes the best butter, she cooks the best kail,
And she bakes the best bread wi the verra same meal;
An' I think, if I wed her, ye needna tak fear
That the lands o' the Lonzies would lang lack an heir.'

'Would it tend to oor credit,' his fair cousin said,
'To mak her yer leddy, your ain servant maid?
Could ye no think the like o' Miss Lindsay or me
A bride to the Laird o' the Lonzies micht be?'

'Miss Lindsay's a lassie weel worth oor regaird,
An aiblins she winna refuse,' quoth the Laird,
'Sae I'll stap up to Evlock withooten mair phrase,
An ye'll just gang wi' me and hear what she says.'

What a pity the Laird is so dull! thought Miss Jean,
For certes he doesna uptak what I mean;
I could bite oot my tongue; I had nae woman craft;
To mention Liz Lindsay I'm sure I was daft.

We ask not the miller to lool doon his back
To bear past his ain empty mill the fu sack;
It passes a' reason, ilk body will grant,
Proposin for ithers what we oorsels want.

The Laird stared astonished; Miss Jean lookit kind;
And noo a bright notion flashed through the Laird's mind—
'If that oor fair cousin oor Lady will be,
Another shall ne'er get an offer,' quoth he.

'I wisna just thinkin to change my estate,'
Quoth Jeanie, 'but then, as ye need a helpmate,
And since ye hae fixt yer affection on me,
To please ye, the Lady o' the Lonzies I'll be.'

Leezie Lindsay

This version of the story of Leezie and her mystery suitor is still popular. According to one version of the story, Leezie already had an admirer when Lord Ronald came on the scene. He was the Laird of Longies, an estate neighbouring Evelick.

Will ye gang to the Hielands, Leezie Lindsay,
Will ye gang to the Hielands wi me?
Will ye gang to the Hielands, Leezie Lindsay,
My bride and my darling to be?

Then I spoke to Leezie's auld mither,
And a canty auld body was she.
'Man, if I was as young as my dochter
I wad gang to the Hielands wi thee.'

Then I spoke to Leezie's own sister,
And a bonnie wee lassie was she.
'O, gin I was as auld as my sister
I wad gang to the Hielands wi thee.'

'But to gang to the Hielands wi you, sir,
I dinnae ken how that may be,
For I ken no the land that ye live in,
Nor ken I the lad I'm gaun wi.'

'O, Leezie, lass, ye maun ken little
When you say that ye dinnae ken me;
My name is Lord Ronald MacDonald,
I'm the chief of a Highland degree.'

So she's kilted her coats o' green satin,
And she's kilted them up to her knee,
And she's aff wi Lord Ronald Macdonald,
His bride and his darling to be.

Meg o' Liff
or The Hags o' Hurly Hawkin

On Christmas Eve lang years ago,
A nicht o' frost an' waffs o' snow,
A wondrous deed was done in Liff,

Which gaed the villagers a gliff,
And still remembered is by a',
Wha seventy winters can reca'.
That nicht the sun, large, wild and red,
In anger socht his western bed,
And left ahint dark, gloomy clouds
To hap the earth in lichtless shrouds.
Then frae each cot the cruisie's gleam
Shone 'mid the mirk wi fitful beam:
Yet gaily rose the weavers' sound,
Fast finishing their daily round.

Up frae the loom leaped Johnnie Rough,
A simple bit o' human stuff,
Wha had that nicht, 'mid rack and moil,
Completed forty years o' toil.

His web was dune, and frae his seat
He rose wi joyous heart and feet,
Took off his apron, shook his hair,
And breathed a 'God be thankit' prayer.
Into the kitchen-end he went,
And by the fire sat doon content.

But Meg, his ill-tongued, randy wife,
The plague o' Johnnie's wedded life,
Began to snap and glower and gloom,
And spiered 'Hoo he had left his loom?'

Quoth Johnnie, wi a timid look,
—For Meg's fierce wrath he'd learned to brook—
'It's forty years this very nicht
Since I began the weavin fecht,
I rose this morn afore the sun,
I've wrocht fell hard—the web is done—
And surely, Meg, for aince, ye'll be,
On Christmas nicht, at peace wi me.'
For twenty years puir John had borne
The lash o' Meg's ill tongue and scorn;
Scarce had a day gone ower his head
Since he unto the wretch was wed,
But inwardly he wished that she
Was laid whaur tongues in silence be.
Aft when his meekness roused her ire,
Her temper burst in spurts o' fire;

She'd shak her fist and aftimes tear
A handfu o' his silvery hair,
Or grab his beard or scart his cheeks,
And like a tartar wear the breeks.

Nae children graced their married life
To quell her love for din and strife.
And sae the little theckit cot
Was ca'd in Liff 'that awfu spot.'

Quoth Meg, 'And ye've wrocht forty years,
Ye guid-for-nothing, it appears
It's noo your only heart's desire
To sit and smoke beside the fire;
Ye lazy snool, and will ye dare
To lauch at me! Rise frae that chair!
Awa ye gang and lift your web,
Or else I'll pu your wizzened neb.
Ye winna gang! Ye winna speak!
My sang, I'se gar yer haffets reek.
Rise frae that chair, ye doited coof,
Rise! Rise!'

Wi that, her muckle loof
Struck silent John a fearfu thwack,
That stretched him ower the auld chair back,
And broke his wee, black cutty freen'
Whase head among the ase was seen.

Quate, uncomplainin, John sat still,
And let her rave awa at will:
Higher and higher rose her tongue,
Wild and mair wild her clamour rung,
Her big, projectin cauld grey een
Changed to a hue o' sickly green,
Her upper lip, lang, deep and thin,
Stretched ower her jaw, like birsled skin,
While at her mou weiks, curds o' froth
Hung as the symbols o' her wroth.
And stampin wi her foot she shook
Her neive at John, wha feared to look
Upon the wild she-deevil form,
That ower his heid blew sic a storm.

Calm and demure, he heard it a',

But ne'er an angry word let fa'
In sorrow at her senseless rage:
He bore it as becomes a sage.

The hour o' ten rang frae the clock,
When at the door a sudden knock
Was heard, and then amid the din,
A yellin horde cam rushin in;
Gash-gabbit hags o' hideous shape,
Wi' een ablaze and mous agape,
And sunken chafts and girnin jaws,
And skinny hands that looked like claws.

They seized on Meg wi skirlin roar,
And whisked her through the open door.
Some grabbed her feet wi powerfu grip,
Some on their shouthers raised her up.
Some filled her mou wi brimstane het,
To still the rage that gurgled yet.

Awa they flew like winter wind,
And left the weaver's cot behind,
Nor slackened ocht o' speed until
They stood on Hurly Hawkin hill.
Then on the ground puir Meg they flung,
And round her danced and round her sung:

> 'We've got her noo,
> What shall we do?
> Sisters say!
> We've got her noo on Hurly Hawkin,
> What shall we do?
> Skelp her! Skelp her!
> Nane will help her,
> Skelp her bare for temper brackin.
> Bring the chair,
> Sit her there,
> We will cure her randy talkin,
> This we'll do
> On Hurly Hawkin!'

That nicht on Hurly Hawkin mound,
Blue lowes rose frae the frosty ground,
And frae each lowe a deevil peered,
Wha at the deed the auld hags cheered,

And lauched and girned and squirmed and yelped,
And wi their tails the ground they skelped.

Wi mystic art a backless chair
Rose frae the earth amid a flare,
And clappin hans aroun it stood
The fiercest o' the beldame brood.

While ithers, skilled in tapes and stays,
Stript Meg o' a' her nether claes,
Syne tied her on the ebon chair,
To skelp her wi a vengeance rare.
Beneath their rags o' bronze-like hue,
Each hag's hand dived and quickly drew
A tawse that seemed a soople tongue,
Frae some wild randy lately wrung.

Around puir Meg wi shout and prance,
They danced as only deevils dance,
And wildly waved their arms and tawse,
And hobbed and bobbed and snapped their jaws.

Syne round their victim closing in,
They for a moment quat their din,
While ane, wi a' her micht, cam whack
On Meg's weel-roonded bonnie back.

In quick succession cam the rest,
And gae their blows wi fiendish zest;
Skelp after skelp wi awfu pith
Rang like the hammer o' the smith.

Meg writhed and twisted wi the pain,
And tried to rise, but 'twas in vain;
She tried to speak, alas, her tongue
For aince unto its dwelling clung.

Loud in the cauld nicht-air arose
The music o' the dreadfu blows,
Which quicker, thicker, harder flew,
Until her skin was black and blue.
Oh! 'twas an awfu sicht to see
Sae fair a back sae yerked wi glee:
Sae plump a form sae sadly tanned
By such a foul, unfeelin band.

Wi ilka blow Meg felt a dart
Straucht fleein through her sinfu heart,
Which weel-nigh burst its yieldin wa's,
For words to speak in pity's cause.

But tears! The first she e'er had shed,
Rose frae her heart and heavenward sped,
Then wi a gasp that seemed her last,
She murmured 'John, forgie the past.'

Then every hag stood still and mute,
And hid her tawse beneath her cloot.
They lifted Meg frae aff the chair,
And dressed her wi a kindly air.
Syne shouther-high they bore her aff,
Wi mony a merry shout and laugh.

And as the solemn hour o' twel'
Was ringin frae the auld kirk bell,
Beside her John, asleep in bed,
His heart-changed Meg they deftly laid.

Then doon the dowie Den o' Gray,
The weird hags took their windin way,
And a' was dark and a' was still
On lonely Hurly Hawkin hill.

Next mornin John was proud to see
His Meg as loving as could be:
Yet never kent the reason hoo
Her tongue was sweet and couthy noo.

He never speired, for John was blessed,
And tore the past from oot his breast.
Sae mony happy years o' life
He lived wi Meg, his ain dear wife.

I regret I have been unable to identify the poet responsible for this tour-de-force of Scots comic verse.

Corunna's Lone Shore

Do you weep for the woes of poor wandering Nelly?
    I love you for that, but I love now no more;
All I had long ago lies entomb'd with my Billy,
    Whose grave rises green on Corunna's lone shore.
Oh! they tell me my Billy looked noble when dying,
    That round him the noblest in battle stood crying,
While from his deep wound life's red floods were drying,
    At evening's pale close on Corunna's lone shore.

That night Billy died, as I lay on my pillow,
    I thrice was alarmed by a knock at my door;
Thrice my name it was called in a voice soft and mellow,
    And thrice did I dream of Corunna's lone shore.
Methought Billy stood on the beach where the billow
    Boom'd over his head, breaking loud, long, and hollow,
In his hand he held waving a flag of green willow,
    'Save me, God!' he exclaimed on Corunna's lone shore.

And now when I mind on't, my dear Billy told me,
    While tears wet his eyes, but those tears are no more,
At our parting, he never again would behold me,
    'Twas strange, then I thought on Corunna's lone shore.
But shall I ne'er see him when drowsy-eyed night falls,
    When through the dark arch Luna's tremulous light falls,
As o'er his new grave slow the glow-worm of night crawls,
    And ghosts of the slain trip Corunna's lone shore?

Yes, yes, on this spot shall these arms enfold him,
    For here hath he kissed me a thousand times o'er;
How bewildered's my brain, now methinks I behold him,
    All bloody and pale on Corunna's lone shore.
Come away, my sweetheart, come in haste, my dear Billy,
    On the wind's wafting wing to thy languishing Nelly;
I've got kisses in store, I've got secrets to tell thee,
    Come, ghost of my Bill, from Corunna's lone shore.

Oh! I'm told that my blue eyes have lost all their splendour,
    That my locks, once so yellow, now wave thin and hoar;
'Tis, they tell me, because I'm so restless to wander,
    And from thinking so much on Corunna's lone shore.
But, God help me, where shall I go to forget him,
    If to Father's, at home in each corner I meet him,
The arbour, alas! Where he used aye to seat him,
    Says, 'Think, Nellie, think on Corunna's lone shore.'

And here as I travel all tattered and torn,
  By bramble and briar, over mountain and moor,
Ne'er a bird bounds aloft to salute the new morn,
  But warbles aloud, 'Oh! Corunna's lone shore.'
It is heard in the blast when the tempest is blowing,
  It is heard in the white broken waterfall flowing,
It is heard in the songs of the reaping and mowing,
  Oh, my poor bleeding heart! Oh, Corunna's lone shore!

Andrew Sharpe

A Legend of Inchmichael

Flisk Point lies on the south shore of the Firth of Tay. North, South, East and West
Inchmichael are between Inchture and Glendoick in the Carse of Gowrie. Where
Inchmichael Ha' stood and when it was burned down I have not so far found out
but Spence's poem has the ring of a tale that has been handed down.

It was the middle watch of night:
  A vessel stranded lay,
Near to the bonny birks of Flisk,
  High on a bank in Tay.
The sailors looked east an west,
  An to Inchmichael Ha',
Till far aboon them in the air,
  They saw a fiery ba'.

The meteor blazed, and brighter blazed,
  Till sight could scarce pursue;
Loud crew Inchmichael's milk-white cock:
  It vanished from the view!
The second night, when on the deck
  The sailors watch resumed,
Another fire-ba' in the air
  The swinging shrouds illumed.

And fast it shot alang the sky,
  Till it began to fa'
Adown the welkin rapidly,
Aboon Inchmichael Ha'.
  It quicker flew, and brighter grew,
And seemed to rival day:
  Again the watchful white cock crew—
It dwindled faint away!

153

The captain on the first mate ca'd;
   He answered, 'Here am I!'
'Away then to Inchmichael Ha',
   Yon wonderous bird to buy;
And should they ask its weight in gold,
   The money quickly tell,
And bring to me the gifted bird,
   For I would like it well.'

At dawn of day the trusty mate
   Was at Inchmichael Ha',
An' he has bought the milk-white cock
   That scared the fiery ba'.
Thrice leaped the captain on the deck—
   A happy man was he:
'My bark shall never be a wreck
   While ye're on board wi me.'

And aye he straiked the milk-white bird,
   And high his worth extolled:
'I wadna part wi' thee, my chuck,
   For thrice thy weight in gold.
Twice have we seen a stormy wraith
   Athwart the welkin fly;
Twice at thy crowing, wond'rous bird!
   It skaithless left the sky.'

The third night came—they kept a watch
   To mark what might befa':
Anon the blazing stormy wreath
   Approached Inchmichael Ha'.
And quick it flew, and red it grew,
   Till, with a whizzing sound,
It lighted on Inchmichael Ha',
   And burned it to the ground!

There was nae man within the Ha'
   That saved a coat or shirt;
Nor was there steed within the sta'
   Again wi' saddle girt:
Nor plough nor harrow in the shed
   Mair razed the swarded plain;
Nor were there cattle in the reed
   E'er heard to low again.

Charles Spence

The meteor blazed, and brighter blazed,
Till sight could scarce pursue;
Loud crew Inchmichael's milk-white cock:
It vanished from the view!

The Cawple-Stowp o' Abernyte

Robert Ford, born in Wolfhill in 1846, edited a number of books, the best known of which are *Thistledown*, a collection of Scots humorous anecdotes, and *The Harp of Perthshire*, an anthology of poetry written by poets with a Perthshire connection. Not so well known is *Hame Spun Lays and Lyrics*, his own collected works.

The verses below, a lament for a vanished hostelry, are based on the traditional snatch of rhyme given elsewhere in this book:

> 'The Cawple-Stowp o' Abernyte
> Makes mony a merry man.'

In bygane days, when stills were rife
    —Lang, lang ere F. McKenzie's days—
There sat an inn amang the whins,
    Weel nor'ward on auld Rossie braes,
Whaur Bawkie ser'd sic reamin swats,
    An usquabae aye sae perfite,
The drooths cam miles, led by its wiles—
    The Cawple-Stowp o' Abernyte.

Nae ill e'er cam it cudna cure—
    Sae trowed its converts, ane an a';
Their proferred pill for ilka ill
    Was—'Fill the stowp, an ca' awa!'
An lots fell sick e'en for the cure
    (Gin that's a lee, gie me the wyte);
'Twas honoured fain, there's nae unsayin—
    The Cawple-Stowp o' Abernyte.

Fu fain men grasped it foamin fou,
    An gaily sent it steerin roun,
While Bawky peched at ilka fraught,
    An leered as ilka law'n cam doon.
His health they pledged wi lood guffaw,
    An roused him on his sonsy kyte;
But looder far they roused the jar—
    The Cawple-Stowp o' Abernyte.

Wi waught on waught, tradition tells,
    Thay maist gat twa sheets i' the wind,
An feats o' strength were tried at length,
    An some wid neither haud nor bind,
But tae the green wad ramp an reel,
    An box, an rive, an roar, an flyte,

Tho' nane cud coup, sae gleg's the stoup,
    The Cawple-Stowp o' Abernyte.

Oh! Sic a mystic pooer it owned—
    A talisman for ilka care;
Tho' crushed wi grief, it lent relief—
    Twa moufu's o't, or little mair,
An chiels ne'er kent tae dance or sing,
    Or crook their neives in vogue tae fight,
Wad risk the three, when led tae pree
    The Cawple-Stowp o' Abernyte.

Its fame was lood ower muir an fell—
    A score o' miles in ilka airt;
An some wha cudna reach't on fit
    Were driven till't whiles in a cairt.
The auld, the young, the rich, the puir,
    The rustic hind, the belted knight,
Hae sung its praise on distant braes—
    The Cawple-Stowp o' Abernyte.

But time mair than the whinstone tries,
    An Bawky's Inn has quit the scene;
The mystic stowp sell't at the roup
    For guineas sax or seventeen.
An noo, in Romish antic hall,
    Ought day ye'll see a ferlie sight—
A timmer bicker cased in gowd,
    The Cawple-Stowp o' Abernyte.

'Wow! Sic a change on Rossie braes
    Sin Bawky's Inn was in its prime!'
Sae sechs an aged passerby,
    While musin o' the aulden time,
An wi his staff upo' the sand,
    See!—'Ichabod' he airts tae write,
Syne at the well regales himsel
    An sighs—'Fareweel tae Abernyte!'

But loungin here amang the knowes,
    An listenin o' the tales o' yore,
The routs o' riotous mirth an shame—
    I joy tae think they're kent nae mair;
But halcyon quiet, an douce content,
    An a' that's lo'ed by tastes polite,

Is *only* known, is *only* strewn,
Oot ower the braes o' Abernyte.

Linn-ma-Gray

When the poet Charles Spence was courting his sweetheart, Jeanie Bruce from Evelick, they often climbed to the waterfall of Linn-ma-Gray in the glen behind Fingask. Jeanie's mother did not think Spence was good enough for her daughter and forbade them to marry.

Spence was a mason to trade but at least one writer has hinted that at times he neglected his work for his poetry and the study of nature.

Jeanie died young and although Spence never forgot her and wrote poems on his loss he was later happily married to another, Anne Bisset.

Linn-ma-Gray, I long to see
Thy healthy height and broomy lea,
Whaur linnets lilt, and leverets play
Around the roar of Linn-ma-Gray.

Linn-ma-Gray, when to the street
Crowds follow crowds, in crowds to meet,
I wend my solitary way
To climb the cliffs of Linn-ma-Gray.

Linn-ma-Gray, each mountain spring
From age to age doth tribute bring,
And, rushing onward to the Tay,
Augments the stream of Linn-ma-Gray.

Linn-ma-Gray, up Baron Hill
I've led my Jean wi right goodwill,
An sat an seen the dashing spray
Lash the dark rocks of Linn-ma-Gray.

Linn-ma-Gray, when in yon ha'
The merry wassailers gather a',
In vain their weel-trained bands essay
The minstrelsy of Linn-ma-Gray.

Linn-ma-Gray, an ye were mine
Wi birk an beech, an yew an pine,
An ash an aik, I would portray
The loveliness of Linn-ma-Gray.

Linn–ma–Gray, high on thy crest
The wagtail builds her felty nest,
And down amid the misty spray
The snipe finds hame at Linn–ma–Gray.

Linn–ma–Gray, the cushats cool
Their pinions, fluttering in thy pool,
Where sunbeam never found its way,
Far ben the glack of Linn–ma–Gray.

Linn–ma–Gray, thy hazels green
Lodge the thrush and finch at e'en,
Lodge me, too, at close of day—
I tune my harp at Linn–ma–Gray.

Linn–ma–Gray, anither linn
May hae its beauties, hearts to win;
But never can they wile away
My wish to muse at Linn–ma–Gray.

Linn–ma–Gray, the time has been
When I, unchallenged, here was seen
By those who now may come and say—
'Hence, vagrant, hence from Linn–ma–Gray.'

Linn–ma–Gray, thy cliffs and streams
What though an earthly lordling claims?
I only recognise the sway
Of Nature's God at Linn–ma–Gray.

Linn–ma–Gray, the holy sound
Of music in thy gorge profound
Might well the tyrant challenge stay
For those who muse at Linn–ma–Gray.

Linn–ma–Gray, if I might have
A wish—some friends would dig a grave,
Where they my cauld remains might lay,
Beside the fall at Linn–ma–Gray.

My coronach would be its cry,
Its stream the lack of tears supply,
And soundly till the rising day
I would sleep on at Linn–ma–Gray.

Linn-ma-Gray, a long farewell—
Nae mair thy solitary dell
Shall listen to my roundelay—
Nae mair I visit Linn-ma-Gray.

Megginch

The name is said to have been originally 'Melginch', meaning bare island. Dean Arthur Stanley, Dean of Westminster, visited the castle and wrote these verses:

Bleak, bare and bald an island stood,
Above old Tay's wide weltering flood;
No tree, no shrub, no floweret crowned
The precinct of this barren ground.

But now how changed that dismal scene—
All decked with ever-varying green;
The darksome yew, the gladsome rose,
The alley's shade, the bower's repose.

So still may Melginch rude and bare
Give way to Megginch sweet and fair;
The softened word its story tell
And break its own transforming spell.

For Lack of Gold

These rather self-pitying verses were written by a native of Kilspindie, Adam Austin. He was a cousin of Jean Drummond of Megginch and the two were childhood sweethearts.

He studied medicine and became a doctor in Edinburgh. The two were engaged and then, at a Perth ball in October 1748, Jean met James, Duke of Atholl. He was an older man, a widower, but he swept Jean off her feet, proposed and was accepted. They were wed the following May.

Adam clearly thought she had married Atholl for all the wrong reasons and took it very badly. However, despite his vow never to love again, he was married, in 1754, to Anne Sempill, sister of Lord Sempill, and the two had a large family.

For lack of gold she has left me, O,
And of all that's dear she's bereft me, O;
She me forsook for Athole's Duke,
   And to endless woe she has left me, O.

A star and garter have more art
Than youth, a true and faithful heart;
For empty titles we must part—
   For glittering show she has left me, O.

No cruel fair shall ever move
My injured heart again to love,
Though distant climates I must rove,
   Since Jeanie she has left me, O.

Ye powers above, I to your care
Resign my faithless, lovely fair;
Your choicest blessings on her share,
   Though she's for ever left me, O.

The Hell Pool

The pool lies in the den of the Balthayock Burn near Balthayock Castle, above Glen Carse. The poet, James Beattie, was born at Leetown, near Errol, in 1796. He worked as a stonemason but, according to Robert Ford in *The Harp of Perthshire*, he 'contracted irregular habits and hastened his end (in 1838) by insistent intemperance'. He is buried in St Madoes Kirkyard. 'Dool' means gloom or sadness.

There's nae dool in Hell Pool:
For down the rock the burnie leaps,
And up the cliff the ivy creeps:
The bonny birks they fringe the brae,
Mix'd wi' the hawthorn and the slae.
Wi' dew the cups are ever full
Of violet and daffodil.
Were I a hermit or a sage
Be that gray cave my hermitage.

There's nae dool in Hell Pool
But Nature in her solemn dress
Of solitary loveliness;
How sweet it were at midnight hour,

To sit beside that ancient tower,
When every sound of earth is still,
Save that deep rustling in the hill:
The breathing spirit of the glen,
That wild woods answer back again.

There's nae dool in Hell Pool,
Though dark and deep at sunny noon,
And darker when the sun gaes doon.
Yet here the wailing cushat doo
Sits moaning on the spruce-fir bough.
The blackbird and the mavis fills
The rocky mansion of the hills,
Art thou with sorrow woe begone,
Come here an hour to muse alone.

There's nae dool in Hell Pool.
It is the greenwood's deepest deep,
Where, unseen, thou mayest weep
O'er the errors thou hast done;
While repentance can atone;
Where the dark and eerie gloom
Tells thee of a day of doom.
Then if thou from sin art shriven,
Here thou hast begun thy Heaven.

The Sidlaw Hills

At Sight Of The Cypress Range, Alberta

The writer Joseph Lee is best known for his First World War poems. A journalist in
Dundee, he died in 1949.

The high hills, the low hills,
　The quiet hills o' hame;
It's O, that I were lying there,
Where curlews wild are crying there,
　Far ower the saut sea faem.

The high hills, the low hills,
　Wi' yellow broom aglow;
It's, O, that I were roaming there,
Wi' her, where darkly foaming there,
　The rushing torrents go.

The high hills, the low hills,
    The hills we trod together;
The silver sage-brush groweth here—
But pale to him who knoweth, dear,
    The sight o' purple heather.

O, high hills, O, low hills,
    Ye have my heart in hold;
Where lonely I am dwelling here,
The plains are widely swelling here—
    Give me thy ramparts old.

O, high hills, O, low hills,
    O, fair hills ower the faem;
Where lightly winds are sighing there,
Where high the clouds are flying there,
Where curlews wild are crying there,
It's O, that I were lying there—
    For then were I at hame.

As I Cam Ower Strathmartine's Braes

In her lifetime Mary Brooksbank was best known for her songs and poems of the Dundee jute mills in which she had started work as a young girl. She also had a well-deserved reputation as a left-wing political activist.

Born Mary Soutar in Aberdeen she was brought to Dundee by her parents at the age of eight or nine. She never left the city for any length of time throughout her long and frequently stormy life.

Some confusion set in a few years after her death as to how old she had been and even when she had died. The year was 1978 and she was 80.

Despite her fierce loyalty to Dundee she was a passionate lover of the countryside and her happiest memories were of all too infrequent visits to 'Strathmartine's Braes', Glenshee, the Den of Kirriemuir and other beauty spots.

When I used to visit her council house in Dundee's east end she used to sing me song after song. This one I regard as one of her best. She told me she had once heard a young tinker lad diddling the tune and had put these words to it. They seem to me to encapsulate her love of freedom in its widest sense and of the hills she could see from the end of the road.

It is significant that when she gathered her songs and poems together and published them in book form she titled the collection *Sidlaw Breezes*. It was republished by David Winter and Son in 1982. In the book this song is called 'Love and Freedom', which was her own name for it.

As I cam ower Strathmartine's Braes
  Wha dae ye think I seen,
But a braw young piper laddie
  Cam a-linkin ower the green,
Singin 'Hey, Donal, Ho, Donal,
  Dirrum a doo a day.'

He played a reel an he played a jig,
  An he played a sweet strathspey,
He roosed my hert till its beat kept time
  Tae the tappin o' my tae.
Singin 'Hey, Donal, Ho, Donal,
  Dirrum a doo a day.'

Oh I've nae gowd tae offer ye,
  For I've gaithered little gear,
But we'll hae love and freedom
  Gin ye'll follow me, my dear.
Singin 'Hey, Donal, Ho, Donal,
  Dirrum a doo a day.'

There's gowd on the broom o' the Sidlaw Hills,
  Honey fae the heather sweet.
There's a speckled trout in the hidlin tarn,
  A velvet carpet neath our feet.
Singin 'Hey, Donal, Ho, Donal,
  Dirrum a doo a day.'

Syne he blew up his chanter
  An sic a spring he plays,
So I chose love and freedom,
  Now I wander a' my days.
Singin 'Hey, Donal, Ho, Donal,
  Dirrum a doo a day.'

Sidlaw Breezes

This is the title poem in Mary Brooksbank's book. It is a more mannered piece than the song and shows her in her most serious vein.

Sweet breezes oer the Sidlaws range,
  Kissing the hills good-night,
Lonely, distant, alien and strange
  In the last of the lambent light.
Craigowl looks down from his lofty rock

Like a sage of ancient lore,
Crouching, watchful to guard the folk
    And the homesteads of Strathmore.
In fields and glens dark shadows play,
    Caressing to sleep the dying day.

Oh sweet the winds that vagrant come
    From hilltop, glen and corrie,
Soft, cool winds from the hills of home
    To the exiled whisper their story
And ruffle the grass oer the youthful dead,
    Who died ere they knew living;
While Clova's stars, high overhead,
    Pure clear lights are giving,
And soft spring rains, like women's tears,
    Keep green their turf for remembered years.

The passing years may changes bring
    To these changeless hills they knew,
The echoes of their lives will ring,
    The betrayed, loyal and true.
Men of a future age will tell
    Of the wars of long ago,
And time the ancient legends kill,
    And truth like Sidlaws breezes blow
When the laughter of freedom rings in the glen
    That knew only the toil of the fettered men.

Sidlaw Hills in the smirr o' the rain,
    Draped in its misty veil,
Hiding yourselves from the world's pain,
    Unheeding its sordid tale,
Will some rude blast in future years
    Shatter your ancient peace,
And I who love you see thro' my tears
    Reason triumphant and horror cease?
While I breathe I'll hope I live to see
    Earth's people united in harmony.

The wanton winds a requiem sing
    For the sorrows of long ago,
In twilight woods sweet echoes ring
    From songsters' coverts, nesting low.
From their hopeful songs we borrow
    Fresh joys our hearts to fill

With gladness greet each new morrow,
    With hope triumphant still,
To build a world where men can be
    Freed from war's insanity.

When winter's icy mantle clothes
    Your shoulders, once verdant green,
As warm and safe beneath the snows
    Lies sleeping a life unseen.
So warm within, our hearts lie hid,
    Awaiting the bursting sun,
When the icy hand from our land we rid
    And a wider freedom is won,
The world will listen to Scotland's plea,
    New Wallaces rise to set us free.

Sidlaw breezes, cool my brow,
    Calm my imprudent fears,
My urgent heart is calling now,
    Impatient of the years.
Still the tumult of my breast,
    Oh would I could heedless be
Of knowledge and reason that breed unrest,
    Oh take this chalice from me.
In brotherhood shall east meet west,
    Then heart and soul and mind can rest.

Some Sources Consulted

Katharine M. Briggs, *A Dictionary of British Folk-Tales* (London, 1970-71)

Robert Chambers, *The Threiplands of Fingask* (Edinburgh, 1880)

Arthur B. Dalgetty, *The Church and Parish of Liff* (Dundee, 1940)

Jeremy Duncan, *Perth and Kinross: The Big County* (Edinburgh, 1997)

William Murdoch Duncan, *Newtyle, A Planned Manufacturing Village* (Coupar Angus, 1979)

P.R. Drummond, *Perthshire in Bygone Days* (London, 1879)

Robert Scott Fittis, *Romantic Narratives from Scottish History and Tradition* (Paisley, 1903)

      Chronicles of Perthshire (Perth, 1877)

      Sketches of the Olden Times in Perthshire (Perth, 1878)

Robert Ford, *The Harp of Perthshire* (London, 1879)

      Thistledown (London, 1901)

James Cargill Guthrie, *Scenes and Legends of the Vale of Strathmore* (Edinburgh, 1875)

George Hay, ed. by Fittis, *Tales of Scotland* (Perth, 1845-47)

W Mason Inglis, *Annals of an Angus Parish* (Dundee, 1888)

      An Angus Parish in the 18th Century (Dundee, 1904)

James Knox, *The Topography of the Basin of the Tay* (Edinburgh, 1831)

Alexander Lowson, *Tales and Legends of Forfarshire* (Forfar, 1891)

Stuart McHardy, *Tales of Whisky and Smuggling* (Moffat, 1991)

A Mackay, *Meigle, Past and Present* (Arbroath, 1876)

J.G. McPherson, *Strathmore: Past and Present* (Perth, 1885)

      McMurray's Diamond Jubilee Guide to Alyth and District (Alyth, 1900)

William Marshall, *Historic Scenes in Perthshire* (Edinburgh, 1881)

      Historic Scenes in Forfarshire (Edinburgh, 1875)

A.H. Millar, *Haunted Dundee* (Dundee, 1923)

Lawrence Melville, *The Fair Land of Gowrie* (Coupar Angus, 1939)

      Errol: Its Legends, Land and People (Perth, 1935)

James Myles, *Rambles in Forfarshire* (Dundee, 1850)

Richard Oram, *Angus and the Mearns: A Historical Guide* (Edinburgh, 1996)

Our Meigle Book (Dundee, 1932)

George Penny, *Traditions of Perth* (Perth, 1836)

Adam Philip, *Songs and Sayings of Gowrie* (Edinburgh, 1901)

      The Evangel in Gowrie (Edinburgh, 1911)

      Things Grave and Gay from Gowrie (Dundee, 1916)

      Romance in Gowrie (Dundee, 1923)

R. Macdonald Robertson, *Selected Highland Folktales* (Edinburgh, 1961)

Sir Walter Scott, *Tales of a Grandfather* (Edinburgh, 1828)

Robert Speake, *Kinfauns Castle* (Manchester, 1982)

James M. Strachan (ed.), *From the Braes of the Carse* (Perth, 1898)

D.P. Thomson, *On the Slopes of the Sidlaws* (Perth, 1953)

INDEX